ROB GIBSON was born in Glasgow ɑı
now lives in Evanton, Easter Ross. F
has encompassed both Highland hill
he graduated from Dundee University with a degree in Modern History
and, until 1995, pursued a teaching career in Easter Ross. Through his
love of traditional music he has convened the Dingwall-based Highland
Traditional Music Festival for twenty years and he has sung in several
groups. Currently with the band Ceilidh Ménage, he has performed at
festivals in Scotland and Brittany. He wrote the show *Plaids and
Bandanas* for performance at the Highland Festival of 1998.

Rob's interest in land issues has led to an active political life includ-
ing working for eight years from 1988 as an SNP District Councillor in
Ross and Cromarty. In 2003 he was elected as SNP MSP for Highlands
and Islands, and has been an enthusiastic member of the Environment and
Rural Development Committee. He has contributed to various journals
over the years and has published several books including *The Promised
Land*; *Crofter Power in Easter Ross*; *Toppling the Duke: Outrage on
Ben Bhraggie?* and *Plaids and Bandanas: From Highland Drover to
Wild West Cowboy.*

# The
# Highland Clearances Trail

ROB GIBSON

**Luath** Press Limited

EDINBURGH

www.luath.co.uk

First published by Highland Heritage Educational Trust, 1983
This Edition 2006
Reprinted 2006
Reprinted 2007
Reprinted 2008
Reprinted 2009
Reprinted 2010
Reprinted 2012
Reprinted 2013
Reprinted 2015
Reprinted 2016
Reprinted 2017
Reprinted 2018
Reprinted 2019

ISBN: 978-1-905222-10-0

The paper used in this book is recyclable. It is made from low
chlorine pulps produced in a low energy, low emissions manner
from renewable forests.

Printed and bound by
Bell & Bain Ltd., Glasgow

Map by Jim Lewis

Illustrations by James Dunn and Marilyn Kay

Typeset in 10.5pt Sabon by
3btype.com

*Dedicated to the late Sandy Lindsay who inspired
many to study the effects of the Clearances on modern
Scotland. His posthumous foreword encapsulates
the spirit of this guide.*

## MAPS, HEIGHT & DISTANCE

Ordnance Survey grid references have been checked from 1:50000 editions. Data has been checked at the time of publication. Scotland's historic counties do not fit the current boundaries of local authorities. Since the Land Registers of Scotland are based on the 33 historic counties, this guide follows that model with areas measured in acres. Heights are given in metres as per Ordnance Survey practice and distances are measured in miles as on road signs.

## TRAVEL

Travel around the Highlands and Islands needs to be well planned especially where ferries have to be caught. I have assumed road transport in the main although that can be copied and extended by bike. Rail routes on the north/south spine and eastern and western branches have much to recommend them. The traveller with limited time or budget can benefit from hopscotch ferry tickets by CalMac ferries and rail rover tickets. Bus services and post buses are important social links that reach most corners, though isolated glens are difficult to access by public transport. For all areas of the country you can start with the VisitScotland website at www.visitscotland.com

## ACKNOWLEDGEMENTS

I wish to thank various informants who have given valuable advice over the years in preparing this guide. Frank G Thompson of Stornoway, the late Joseph Mackay of Lairg, Katharine Stewart of Abriachan, Willie Orr of Oban, the late Sandy Lindsay of Kingussie, Dr Ian Glen of Dalnavert, Alan Roydhouse, Bob Mulholland of Farr by Inverness and the late Joan Fraser of Corstorphine deserve particular thanks. Many thanks to James Dunn and Marilyn Kay for the line drawings.

# Contents

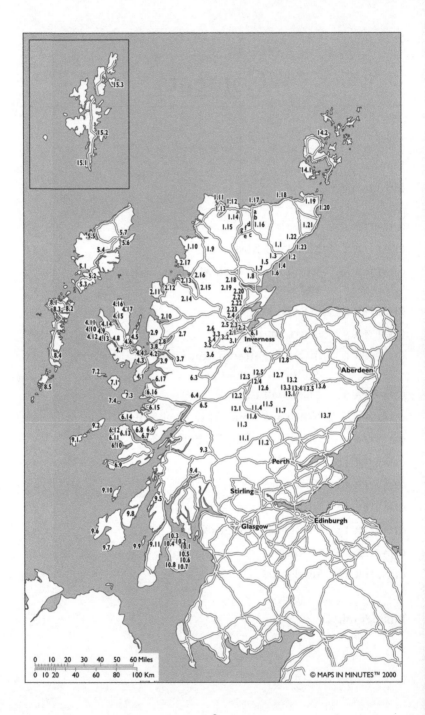

# Map index

# Foreword

THIS BOOK IS A brief but scholarly introduction to the most tragic period in the history of Scotland. It illustrates 'man's inhumanity to man' in that, given powers over their fellow men, those in positions of authority care solely for their own wealth and wellbeing.

This period has real importance in that the Gaelic people were regarded as inferior. The destruction of their language, culture and way of life was regarded as no more important that that of any native people in the British Empire. Recently the *Daily Telegraph*, a long-established English newspaper, through one of its columnists, the late Auberon Waugh, made this aspect very clear. I am pleased that Rob Gibson should bring this to our notice.

It is a simple matter of fact that the education establishment choses to ignore this chapter in our history, and demonstrates that Scottish education in this matter has failed our communities. This book goes some way to redress this lack of information. In practical terms those interested in the reality of historical crime can follow the Clearances Trail to the various significant locations described here.

*Se Firinn Is Ceartas a Sheasas* – Truth and justice will prevail.

*Sandy Lindsay*
Kingussie

# Introduction – Clues to the Highlands of today

BY 1819 THE final stages of forced upheaval that was designed to modernise the Sutherland Estates were about to take place. Patrick Sellar, the incoming sheep farmer, wrote to James Loch, chief factor, with his triumphant opinions:

> It had induced already a most astonishing effect on the minds of the aborigines. Several – I believe most of the half-pay captains are meditating or have already planned their flight, and the common people are so effectively cowed that, since Martinmas, here, to the wonder of all my people, [we have not] lost one sheep by theft! . . . we shall move steadily forward at Whitsunday, and shall make your Clearance of the hill. . . once and for all.

It is little wonder that the grip held by the Highland Clearances on Scottish minds is as strong now in the 21st century, as it was when a bragging 'Improver' like Patrick Sellar discussed his business plans, or the people forced from their homes first told their heart breaking story.

Since the 1850s most Scots have lived in towns and many have taken the emigrant boat, train or bus to other lands, by choice or by necessity. Looking back on the Clearances engenders discomfort, anger and puzzlement. This is especially so since modern journalists and historians have sought to explain why Scots, who were seen as the most enterprising of people in the 19th century, saw significant numbers from their midst being hounded, leaderless, from their ancient homelands in the Gaelic north and west Highlands and Islands.

Dispossession and removal seems to be something confined today to trouble spots on other continents, yet some commentators in our own country have consistently denied the very core concerns people have about the Highland Clearances, or indeed, that they ever occurred. The rude awakening of modern thinking to explain the Clearances was written by John Prebble, the English journalist-cum-historian in the 1960s. His popular trilogy *Culloden*, *The Highland Clearances* and *Glencoe* shook academic complacency to its roots. He was joined by his contemporary, Ian Grimble, who was by contrast a distinguished, trained historian. James Hunter, Allan MacInnes, Tom Devine and Eric Richards and others since have expanded our vision as the old texts of 18th and 19th centuries were dusted down and new light shone on murky places.

University-based historians insisted that people had always been moved here and there by their landlords and chiefs. After all, the homes of 100,000 poor folk were swept aside to drive the railways into central London; surely it was all for the best? Hadn't the Borders and Lowlands of Scotland been modernised by removals, following the pattern of the prolonged English enclosures begun in Tudor times? This did not explain the Highland situation that was characterised by such swift changes, the destruction of an ancient Gaelic culture and the consequent arrival of sheep ranching and vast Victorian deer forests. The new order left no place for the native people and abused their land. Of course this same colonialism was going on all over the world at that time. Indeed some Highlanders were amongst the worst abusers of other native peoples. Of this there is ample proof, but with the growing doctrine of superior and inferior peoples amongst the empires of Europe and America, Highlanders often chose to grab what they could abroad.

Nevertheless there are glowing exceptions. A lad of five years from Baldoon, Ardross accompanied his father on business and witnessed the clearance of Glencalvie in May 1845. In his adult-hood, as second son of the farm, he emigrated to New Zealand. John MacKenzie remembered the reasons for Glencalvie when he became a minister in the Liberal government of 1890. He led the campaign for laws to be passed that ensured no big estates would gobble up the land to the detriment of family farmers. His record, as with all administrations, was less sound regarding Maori lands in North Island, but not so grossly exploitative as the local Tories.

Modern studies in social history helped fuel the ferment of student uprisings and the anti-war movements of 1968. Historian

EP Thompson, in his groundbreaking book of 1963, *The Making of the English Working Class*, chronicles the effects of modernisation and capitalism on the working classes in England. Simply put, he answered major questions about how industrialisation affected the lives of ordinary folk. He carefully noted the different experience of Scots from the English workers and their families especially prior to 1820. But the Highland experience was a world further apart.

The rise of Scottish political consciousness in the 1960s coincided with this age of enquiry into social history and brought new analysis to bear on the effects on Scotland of being an engine room of the British Empire. Questions as to why so many Scots had emigrated to the far corners of the Earth pointed back to the disproportionate losses of people from the Highlands and Islands that accelerated from the mid-18th century onwards. Indeed the consequences of this continued drain were proving a running sore for British governments in the 1960s. Emigration and lack of work were seriously disabling and depopulating large areas of rural and also urban Scotland.

Until the 1960s Scottish universities had played a less than glorious part in analysing the Highland problem. The much-heralded 1969 book by TC Smout, *A History of the Scottish People 1560-1830*, seems to have made erroneous judgements about the plight of the Highlanders. It contained part of a quotation of Thomas Pennant, yet Prof. Smout excluded the explanation of the people's plight offered by the 18th century Welsh naturalist, antiquary and traveller who had visited Sutherland at a critical time:

> They are content with little at present, and are thoughtless of futurity; perhaps on the motive of Turkish vassals, who are oppressed in proportion to their improvements. Dispirited and driven to despair by bad management, crowds are now passing, emaciated with hunger, to the Eastern coast.

Prof. Gordon Donaldson, former head of the Scottish History Department of Edinburgh University, decried John Prebble's work in a *Sunday Standard* interview by James Hunter on 3 May 1981 as, 'contributing a great deal to the state of mind of left wing agitation'.

Donaldson continued, 'I am 68 now and until recently I had hardly heard of the Highland Clearances. The thing has been blown up out of all proportion.' Donaldson and in his turn Smout were appointed as Historiographers Royal for Scotland.

While both Donaldson and Smout acknowledged chronic economic problems of living in the tough climate and terrain of the Highlands and Islands, they did not analyse the economic impact of introducing the potato that increasingly became the staple food of so many. They minimised the effects of shovelling the native people to the barren coasts from fertile inland straths. They ignored the Highlands' lower than average population increase or the uncertain and truncated development of cattle, whisky, kelp, fishing, weaving, quarrying, military service and iron smelting. Neither assessed the impact of conflict between the dominant values of Hanoverian British rule of progress and order on the apparently backward pastoral Celtic society. Parts of it dared to defy the regime for a century, sometimes attracting the Scottish elite to the cause, until the final pacification in 1746. Culloden, the disastrous last pitched battle on Scottish soil, was a breaking point that induced the passage of repressive legislation on a new scale of thoroughness. Neither historian referred to the role of blatant racism in 19th and early 20th century Britain against the 'backward' Celts, who were despised in Ireland and treated in Scotland during the potato blight as requiring moral uplift through regular manual labour.

Unsurprisingly Scottish schools shied away from studying the Clearances until Standard Grades in the 1980s introduced a patch study of the key period. Previously Highland evictions appeared to have no significant part in the greater tale of British history, so they were ignored. Surprisingly most Scots came across oblique references to Highland unrest, if at all, through a focus on the Irish Land League and demands for Irish Home Rule that eventually rocked the British Empire. So it was left to popular culture to remember the people's past. The left-wing political theatre group 7:84 who performed John McGrath's ceilidh play *The Cheviot, the Stag and the Black, Black Oil*, which swept the Highlands in 1973, argued that until economic power, land and other resources were in the people's hands the exploiters would prevail. This coincided with massive Scottish oil finds in the North Sea and led more and more Scots to agree.

In November 1981 a group called Highland Heritage promoted an alternative view of the Highlands to the castles, tartan and heather image. They produced a Clearances Trail Guide leaflet listing places to visit where the glens were denuded of people over the preceding 200 years and where the crofters fought back. A rebuff from the local Tourist Board officer stated, 'although the leaflet is not of a party political nature, it is clearly controversial and inappropriate for distribution from our information centres.' Highland Heritage's offer to supply it to the tourist information centre in Inverness was emphatically rejected and the subsequent *Glasgow Herald* story headlined 'Highland tourist offices ban leaflet explaining Clearances'. In an editorial comment entitled, 'Unsuitable for tourists' the *Herald* leader writer felt that the Scottish Tourist Boards's excuse that the leaflet was too 'controversial' and therefore 'inappropriate' for tourists was 'feeble'. Nevertheless the paper concluded, 'the Clearances may have been economically and historically inevitable but that does not dilute their dark and tragic aspect which still moves our anger and compassion.'

What could induce myopia and taint of political bias among those who would suppress the story? For much of the century the marginal nature of Highland life was treated as a footnote in general histories. Wilful misrepresentation was the mark of mainstream academics regarding the work composed by Gaelic poets and folk memory. The voices of ordinary people in the Crofting Counties were easily ignored.

The Victorian craze for sport in the wild Highlands saw the natives as ghillies, servants and deer watchers and consequently led to the destruction of peasant life. But a remarkable fightback using the Irish Land League model came about in the early 1880s and led to some security of tenure for small tenants. Many academics still ignored the testimony given to Royal Commissioners in communities all around the north in 1883 and 1893. The distinguished historian Rosalind Mitchison dismissed the recollections of men like Angus

MacKay of Strathy Point for the Napier Commission in 1883. MacKay had described conditions in Strathnaver before the Sellar Clearances where 'the people had plenty of flocks of goats, sheep, horses and cattle, and they were living happy.' Mitchison continues, 'the picture is clearly rubbish, and it is the duty of the historian to label rubbish as such when he meets it.'

Thanks to painstaking study by Iain Grimble, contemporary evidence of 18th century life in north Sutherland was presented. His witnesses include the poet Rob Donn MacKay; the testimony of emigrants at their point of departure to port officials; the travellers' tales of Episcopal bishop Richard Pococke; the observations of naturalist Thomas Pennant and the memoirs of the son of the Kildonan parish manse the Rev. Donald Sage. They all swelled a new stream of consciousness because they had seen a society on the brink of being sundered as it had never been since the arrival of the Vikings in the 9th century.

The results of the economic slump after Napoleon's defeat in 1815 were falling incomes and fewer economic opportunities. By the mid-1840s the dependence on one strain of potato by three-quarters of the West Highland population meant that the inevitable wind-borne blight devastated this monoculture. Soon landlords were calling for a clear-out of the remaining Highland population. Such policies were advocated by civil servants recruited to the famine relief operations. An Anglo-Celt, Sir Charles Trevelyan, viewed the Highland Celts as racially inferior, if not as inferior as the Irish who were 'turbulent and blood thirsty'. Of a 'reformed' Cornish background and a pious Christian of the 'Clapham Sect', he recruited men of similar beliefs such as the third son of the Colonsay laird, Sir John McNeill and the Celtic historian William Skene. The former deplored the dependence of the poor on charity as it blinded the victims to their need to support themselves. The latter may have admired ancient Celtic culture but blamed the crofters for their own plight.

Modern research on the Irish Famine of 1845–51 prompted Prof. Tom Devine, then teaching at Strathclyde University, to write *The Great Highland Famine: Hunger, Emigration and the Scottish*

*Highlands in the Nineteenth Century.* It won the 1991 Saltire Prize and the *Glasgow Herald* Book of the Year. It also won grudging praise from Prof. Smout in *The Economic History Review:*

> It is based on an extraordinary volume of papers, which have survived for a majority of the great estates of the area, and on meticulous use of government, charity, and census manuscripts. The outcome is a new understanding of the early Victorian Highlands, presented with a wealth of detail and scrupulous and subtle judgement.

But Smout conceded:

> . . . sometimes it confirms what others have surmised on more slender evidence: often it tells the tale properly for the first time and offers basic revision of accepted ideas.

Crucially for those who denied that the Clearances were important, the hard analysis of scholars like Devine confirmed the widespread nature of the problem. Devine later summed up the 18th century Highland crisis in *The Scottish Nation 1700–2000:*

> Such pools of indigenous enterprise as did exist were inhibited in a variety of ways. The destruction of the old order, resettlement and rental inflation combined to produce a context of profound insecurity that was not conducive to small tenant investment.

He went on to chart the enforced and assisted emigration of which peaked from Scottish ports in 1852, swelled by Irish emigrants travelling via Scotland. It is still very hard to get an accurate picture of the destinations of Highlanders. However the general Scottish emigration trail led around half to the USA, a third to Canada and the remainder to Australia and New Zealand. Gradual recovery after the famine years of 1845–51 for those who remained was based on fragile economic factors. Devine again:

> The entire structure depended ultimately on five factors: the recovery of the prices gained for Highland black cattle; a steep

fall in world grain prices in the 1870s and 80s; a continued expansion of steam navigation in the western Highlands; the growth of the indigenous fishing industry; and a further increase of temporary migration and casual employment.

A fishing slump added to agricultural depression in the early 1880s to produce not despair but an organised resistance across the Highlands to demand security of tenure. The evidence given by crofters and cottars to the Napier Commission in 1883 inevitably dipped into the woes of a century of Clearance but it also showed outbreaks of resistance from the time of the Great Sheep Drive in Ross-shire in 1792 and in every decade thereafter. Still Patrick Sellar's son Thomas could spring to his father's defence as the great 'improver' when he tried to counter the crofters' claims. His book *The Sutherland Evictions of 1814* regurgitated the landlord's perspective. Soon afterwards the distinguished historian Andrew Lang penned the entries for the prestigious *National Dictionary of Biography* that whitewashed James Loch and Patrick Sellar. Lang was Sellar's grandson.

It came as little surprise that reactionary writings have continued to be vigorously challenged in the past 25 years. Yet reactionaries still surface. When a campaign was launched to remove the statue of the Duke of Sutherland from Ben Bhraggie it attracted worldwide comment. Sandy Lindsay and Peter Findlay lodged an outline planning application for its removal and replacement with a Celtic cross. The nine metre high, stone Duke was to be re-erected in the gardens of the French Renaissance-style chateau of Dunrobin Castle. Though the Highland Council turned down the applicants, they did agree to the need for interpretation of what the visitor was seeing when they trudged up from Golspie to inspect the 'Mannie'. Few if any residents of Golspie actually knew why the statue took four years to reach completion in 1838. Yet they are inordinately proud of the stone monster on their skyline. The most vitriolic reaction to the statue's removal came from Auberon Waugh, in the *Daily Telegraph* of 3 February 1996. He blistered the paper in denouncing the 'whingers' who threatened it. He wrote that few were prepared:

. . . to speak up for the great Duke of Sutherland, whose Highland Clearances might well rank as the first liberal or enlightened act by any major landlord in the history of Scotland. The conditions of the peasants squatting on poor land, which they were too drunk and too lazy to farm, was totally abject. The land could not support any form of agriculture beyond the lightest sheep cropping. They lived amid piles of their own excrement in godless squalor, breeding like rabbits, drinking like fishes and dying like flies. When the Duke moved these wretched, murdering drunken people to better land on the coast, and restored the Highlands to their pristine beauty, he was as much inspired by simple philanthropy as he was by aesthetic, hygienic or mercenary considerations. Those with sufficient ability stayed on as fishermen and farmers. Those without, moved West again to Canada and the United States. But the Scots have never forgiven him for rescuing them from their squalor. There is even an appeal to knock down the magnificent 106-foot monument on Ben Bhraggie, where the Duke still stands as monarch of all he surveys. They plan to replace the statue with something 'more fitting' to commemorate the people who were moved, blinding and swearing, from their hovels, to a new life elsewhere. It is a monument to the perpetual whinge.

Most recently, in *Wild Scots: Four Hundred Years of Highland History*, the Tory devotee of free market capitalism Scots historian Michael Fry, he denies that the Clearances were widespread or very important in the greater scheme of modernisation. There was surplus population; Highlanders had been used to seeking work elsewhere for centuries; opportunities in the colonies beckoned. He praised the modernising lairds who took advantage of higher rents as a result of top prices achieved from sheep farming. Raising four times the profit compared to the old cattle economy, would anyone have done differently? If you look at the Viking peasant farms of Scandinavia, there's an immediate and stunning contrast, where land is much more evenly divided. As of long-held right, peasant farmers thrive with forestry, crops and animals all providing a steady income in a country that supports its community life in the countryside.

Undoubtedly Scots flourished in the New World. Letters from emigrants beckoned their unfortunate relations and friends back home to visit them with tales of good harvests and the absence of estate factors to interfere. Even so the struggle to cross the seas and to get established took a toll that is measured in tens of thousands. At Grosse Ile, the quarantine station on the St Lawrence River, 5,200 immigrants are buried in mass graves from the influx in the 1830s and 1840s. They died there of fever, weakened by starvation before setting off. The disease-ridden ships, the harsh North American winters and the hostility of Indians, French and Méti were compounded by hard-bargaining businessmen who screwed every penny they could from the new arrivals. If you had the right connections things could go well.

Unfortunately most of the people sent abroad in the 19th century were already in straitened circumstances. In 1879 after a century of rapid urbanisation and unprecedented emigration, Robert Louis Stevenson wrote *From the Clyde to California*, describing the fate of his fellow emigrants who crossed the Atlantic:

> We were a company of the rejected; the drunken, the incompetent, the weak, the prodigal, all who had been unable to prevail against circumstances in the one land, were now fleeing pitifully to another; and although one or two might still succeed, all had already failed. We were a shipful of failures, the broken men of England.

The Highland Clearances Trail reaches many places that lost their communities, where people left in small groups, in families and in trepidation for the future. Removals ended generations of settlement, tens of thousands were affected, although most of these sad events passed without incident, the question has been raised by today's commentators as to people's rights to have a home place immune from such eviction. That's why people today want to see the localities from which so many were cleared for an uncertain life in our cities and abroad. It is a complicated story, some of it is well documented, and much is little recorded. In 1755 over half of Scots lived on land north of a line from the Clyde to the Tay. Today a fifth of Scots live in the north. So the story is far from complete. Gross overcrowding in Central Scotland and clan names scattered around the world are a direct result.

# CHAPTER I

# Sutherland and Caithness

THE FIERCE WINDS of economic change began to blow on the northern mainland of Scotland with the introduction in the 1780s of hardy Cheviot sheep by Sir John Sinclair of Ulbster. He hoped to integrate them with existing agriculture. But the writing was on the wall. It soon became clear how landlords would respond to the stark economic fact that returns from the Cheviot promised to increase profits by a factor of six over income from tenants. The Sutherland estates organised the largest planned programme of Clearances anywhere in Scotland that set the benchmark for 'Improvers' in the Highlands.

An introduction to scenes that will be described in this tour can be viewed by driving inland from Helmsdale (ND 025153) in east Sutherland. Driving along a single track road through the Strath of Kildonan on the A897 is a 20 mile journey north-west from Helmsdale to Kinbrace. Each bend in the road reveals a landscape of stunted birches, bracken infested hillsides, ruins of old houses and sheep droppings in every lay-by. Hidden behind the tranquil scene is a troubled history. In 1812 there was resistance by local people to planned 'improvements' by the Countess of Sutherland, and the Dunrobin Castle administration backed off temporarily. But the countess, who owned nearly all of Sutherland, was married to the richest man in England, the great improving laird, the 2nd Marquis of Stafford. The noble couple were not to be thwarted for long in their zeal to transform her domain into a 'modern' profitable estate. The ruthless Strathnaver Clearance of 1814 was effectively a blueprint for clearances of tenants to make way for sheep in Kildonan and many other inland straths from where in the following eight years, some 7,000 people were removed.

East and West Helmsdale were originally set up as planned

Clearance villages to house the displaced inland dwellers and introduce them to gainful employment such as fishing and new weaving techniques. Helmsdale Harbour (NC 029151) was the showpiece improvement.

The Strath of Kildonan is associated with a secret champion of the oppressed, the Rev. Donald Sage. In *Memorabilia Domestica* that was published many years later, he remembered in his youth travelling from his father's manse beneath Beinn Dobhain and witnessing houses still burning, a full week after the Strathnaver evictions. Reading *Memorabilia Domestica* we can understand the pressure on him; in these Highland parishes the laird appointed the minister and expected his support for the improvements.

The Timespan Heritage Centre, Bridgend, Helmsdale contains an interpretative exhibit on the Kildonan Clearances, a locally initiated project. The curious inclusion of a Barbara Cartland Exhibit only serves to emphasise the continued influence of the hunting and shooting lairds, of whom the late romantic novelist was a scion. Their shooting lodges provide the main employment in the near-empty strath.

Gartymore Land League cairn (ND 013154) was erected in 1981, around a mile on steep township roads from the Bridge Hotel, Helmsdale. It marks the centenary of the first branch of the Sutherland Association, one of the parent bodies of the Highland Land League that eventually had 15,000 members. Five Crofters' MPs were elected at the 1885 and 1886 elections, the first in which the male rural tenant had the vote, and for the first time giving the people of the Highlands a real say in Parliament. Sutherland Constituency returned Angus Sutherland in the second election, after he had been narrowly outvoted in 1885 by the then Marquis of Stafford. The 1886 Crofters' Holdings (Scotland) Act, passed by the short-lived Gladstone government, is a lasting memorial to the Highland Land League and the Crofters' MPs. The Land League cairn is inscribed with the biblical text, 'They laid the foundations that we might build thereon'. Local people built it in the spirit of defiance of the Land Leaguers, as a visible reminder, and indictment, of what is wrong with the Highlands to this day.

If you drive south along the A9 (T) through Portgower – one of the many new settlements created and named by the Stafford dynasty – the narrow coastal plain opens out somewhat at Lothmore (NC 964115) and Lothbeg (NC 943105) whose ancient communities were cleared in 1819 by the Sutherland family to make bigger farms. An approving account of these clearances is given in Alexander Sutherland's *A Summer Ramble in the North Highlands*, published in 1827. Sutherland praised Lady Stafford's efforts by dint of substantial expenditure to 'reverse the decree of nature'. Yet he provides this description of the journey north of Brora through an area where 67 families had just been removed:

> All was silence and desolation. Blackened and roofless huts, still enveloped in smoke, articles of furniture cast away, as of no value to the houseless and a few domestic fowls, scraping for food among hills of ashes, were the only objects that told us of man. A few days had sufficed to change a countryside, teeming of the cheeriest sounds of rural life, into a desert. Man the enlivener of this scene, was gone – gone into the wilderness, like our first parents, a pilgrim and an exile; and the spirit of desolation sat exulting on the ruins of his forsaken abode. It is impossible for a stranger, with such a scene before him, to keep his mind totally free from prejudice.

Follow the A9 through Brora. In nearby Uppat Wood is the estate's monument (NC 873018) to James Loch, the Sutherland family commissioner who oversaw the modernisation of Sutherland. The monument is not visible from the road. Two miles on, the road reaches the gates of Dunrobin Castle (NC 851010). The crowstep gables of the old Scots castle were hidden in a lavish creation based on a French chateau and planned by the first Duke of Sutherland to be the 'Versailles of the North'. It was completed after his death in 1850. Some years ago it was the scene of Clan Sutherland's international gatherings. Now it is a museum to Victorian extravagance, open from May to September. Lord Strathnaver, today's heir to the 90,000 acre Sutherland Estates, has tried to promote the castle as a local cultural centre.

Beinn a'Bhragaidh, or in its anglicised form, Ben Bhraggie, a

394 m hill, lies one and a half miles north-west of Golspie, over-looking the village and Dunrobin Castle. It is the site (NC 814009) of a huge statue of the 1st Duke of Sutherland. Chantrey made a ten foot high model in marble from which his assistant Theakston used as a template for the Ben Bhraggie monument. Patrick Sellar proposed it be erected on top of 961 m Ben Klibreck (NC 584299), in the middle of the duke's domain, with this inscription:

> This spot, Her Grace Elisabeth the 1st Duchess of Sutherland, permitted to the Tenantry of the Estate of Sutherland, to conse-crate to the memory of George Granville Leveson Gower, her husband, the much beloved Father of His People.

The estate management declined both of Sellar's suggestions and decided on Ben Bhraggie and a far less emotive inscription. James Loch sought subscribers from every one of a 'grateful tenantry' but the money came largely came from his own class, among them Patrick Sellar who donated £40 in the total of £1,430 16s 8d.

It is said that the duke's widow criticised the rough finish of the shoulders of the statue, but was assured by Chantrey, '. . . t'would only be gulls and crows observe the upper surfaces once the statue was erected.' It can be seen from a great distance with its back turned to land the duke cleared. The best approach is from Golspie High Street car park at Fountain Road and on foot via the recently improved footpath starting at Rhives Farm (NC 828003).

The 9 m high statue sits on a 19 m plinth of sand-stone quarried on the hill. It has been subject to many 'demolition' rumours in its 150-year existence. In October 1995 activists lodged a planning application to remove the statue from the plinth and re-erect it in the garden of Dunrobin Castle. The area planning committee rejected the plan but the debate about the con-troversial statue reverberates around the globe.

Statue of the 1st Duke of Sutherland on Ben Bhraggie

Augustus Grimble gives the sports fisherman's view of the monument in *The Salmon Rivers of Scotland* (1913):

> The angler on the lower reaches of the Fleet is daily looked down on by the monument on Golspie Hill. It was built in honour of the same duke who, at his own expense, emigrated so many of his crofters greatly to their own benefit; the tradition relates that after the putting up of the monument some wag scribbled on its base the following lines:
>
> There once was a great Duke of Sutherland,
> Whose crofters were fond of their motherland,
> But to each one he said,
> Your passage is paid,
> And off you must go to some other land. . .
>
> I would not vouch for the truth of this story, but at any rate the lines are rather funny.

The A9 south of Golspie reaches The Mound (NH 778983), a massive earth embankment and bridge that dams and crosses the boggy Strath of Fleet, constructed c. 1815 by the Sutherland Estates as an aid to their Improvements. Designed by Thomas Telfer its completion was supervised by a very impatient Patrick Sellar who was a sub-factor and aspiring sheep farmer. Along with other flock masters in the North he destroyed the old cattle society across the county. Turning west on the A839 via Rogart, the road passes through an area that has clung to the crofting system to this day. It is 14 miles to Lairg, where a choice of four routes north-west beckons; via the A838 along to Laxford Bridge; via the A836 to Altnaharra continuing to the Kyle of Tongue and north-west via a minor road to Strath More and Loch Eriboll; north-east on the B873 to Syre and the B871 via Strathnaver to the north coast; or drive 33 miles west on the A839 from Lairg to Rosehall, then follow the A837 along Strath Oykell to Ledmore and on to Inchnadamph in Assynt. This scattered township sits in a lush limestone valley amidst spectacular scenery capped by the sharp outline of 731 m Suilven and 846 m Canisp to the west and 998 m Ben More Assynt to the east.

Seeing the way the Sutherland Estate managers were inclined, before 1812 Assynt tacksmen started to clear their sub-tenants to bring in sheep farming. The new plans under William Young and later George Gunn were achieved with less rancour or open dissent in 1812, 1819, 1820 and 1821. Homes in Assynt were not burned, but the arrangements for learning fishing or kelp-making were not well-received by the sub-tenants and small farmers who had been used to the rhythms of the cattle economy. They were in no mood to be made over into off-shore fishermen with all its dangers and uncertainties and the managers complained 'it seems there is no overcoming their indolence'.

The Napier Commission that investigated the condition of the crofting population in 1883 was presented with a list of 48 cleared townships in Assynt. A typical story comes from Achna-heaglais, or Kirkton of Assynt, cleared in 1819. Two adjacent town-ships, Camore and Cuilean, contained 143 people. The minister and school-teacher were not evicted, only they and 15 others were allowed to remain while 129 people were cleared to overcrowded plots laid out by the Sutherland estates on the already crowded north Assynt coast, mainly at Clashnessie (NC 055308], Achnacarnin (NC 045320) and Culkein (NC 038331). Achnaheaglais is not on any map; the name vanished like its people. The kirk at Inchnadamph (NC 249220), with its graveyard and remains of a pre-Reformation chapel, was once at the centre of a populous fertile district.

Continue along the A837 for 12 miles to Lochinver, and thence by the B869 to reach another rugged part of north Assynt, and a string of coastal crofting townships including Stoer and Drumbeg. In 1992 this 21,132 acre estate was dramatically repossessed by the Assynt Crofters' Trust after a successful worldwide appeal to back their community purchase. Trust chairman, Allan MacRae, whose great-grandfather was cleared 'at the point of a sword' from Ardvar (NC 172340) to make way for a sheep farmer, led the new crofting 'landlords' to their revival plans for their homeland that took effect in February 1993.

Removals in 1840 at Oldany (NC 100328) were achieved peace-ably, but in 1851 strong resistance at Knockan (NC 215105) and

Elphin (NC 214117) caused planned clearances to be abandoned. Resistance to injustice has an honourable place in Assynt history. An eviction in 1878 led to unrest. Overcrowding in the area of Clashmore (NC 034311) forced many families, including that of Hugh Kerr, to deforce sheriff officers. Kerr, dubbed the 'Assynt Robin Hood', led the life of an outlaw in defiance of eviction orders issued in 1887.

Further along the B869 past Drumbeg, rejoin the A894 near Unapool (NC 237328), from where nine households were moved to Achnacarnin and seven to America! Crossing the Kylesku Bridge you enter the large parish of Eddrachillis, where in the 1790s during the first flush of sheep farm development, it seems 50 families were removed from their farms, without provision for their wellbeing.

It is 20 miles to Laxford Bridge junction and a further 20 miles to Durness on the north coast. Balnakeil House (NC 393687) is on a sign-posted minor road west of the village. In the nearby cemetery you can find the grave of Rob Donn MacKay (1714–78) whose work is a memorial to 18th century life in Reay. Balnakeil House was a home of the Lords of Reay, whose dynasty sold out the last of their lands to the Sutherlands in 1829. It is being considered for renovation today as a Clan MacKay world archive and museum. The predatory Sutherlands had done nothing to help their struggling landed neighbours. When Strathnaver was sold in 1800, Durness and Tongue were left as the last MacKay strongholds.

From Cape Wrath, to Balnakeil Bay, round Loch Eriboll, across the Moine to the Kyle of Tongue and on to Torrisdale Bay at the mouth of the River Naver, is a sparsely populated land. It consists of deep straths and glens whose hills, such as Arkle 757 m, and Foinavon 908 m, are familiar names to racegoers, due to the race-horse-owning Dukes of Westminster, who bought the sporting estate from the Sutherland family and now own more of the county than the Dunrobin dynasty. As late as the mid-18th century the Lords of Reay presided over this vast deer-hunting ground in what, to the minds of Lowlanders, was this remote province. It boasted a thriving Gaelic-speaking culture whose luminaries included the bard Rob Donn and collectors of Highland airs and pibroch.

The Durness area came under Sutherland ownership around 1829 and systematic Clearances took place in 1841. Continue east from Durness on the A838 for three miles to Ceannabeinne (NC 439656). It forms a ruined township straddling the main road. Resistance by women of the area to expel sheriff officers was futile. The expulsions in the area were completed in 1841. Three miles further on at Laid (NC 413590) the survival of holdings marked out on the poorest of land is amazing. While the Crofting Acts helped stabilise such a fragile community, sheep grazing land was resumed by the laird in 1936, thanks to a legal technicality. A solicitor noted that the township was, 'in a remote district far removed from stock markets and their holdings are of a class so poor that they are probably unrivalled in that respect'.

Fifteen miles further east at Hope, a little to the east of Loch Eriboll on the A838, take the unclassified road about ten miles inland to Alltnacaillich (NC 458456). This former settlement was sited at the foot of a steep escarpment that rises to 927 m, making Ben Hope the most northerly Munro in Scotland. According to the Reay Papers, this area of Strathmore was cleared in 1819. Flushed with his success at clearing Strathnaver and Kildonan, Patrick Sellar urged Lord Reay to promote more sheep farms on his land. By 1819, one hundred able-bodied young people had been shipped from Loch Eriboll for Ontario. In dreadful winter storms, all were lost. Another emigrant ship from the area in the same decade ran ashore on Orkney. A descendant of one of those shipwrecked, who later lived in Northampton, England, recalled that her great-grandmother gave birth to her grandfather on the beach.

The house stones of Alltnacaillich were used to make foundations for the present road, which disguises the size of previous habitations. Nearby, Dundornagill Broch (NC 457450), the best-preserved broch in Sutherland, is a testament to the ancient civilisation that inhabited the strath till the imperative of sheep farming cleared the people. The famous Gaelic bard Rob Donn MacKay began his working life here as a herdboy at the Muisel home of Iain MacEachainn, the MacKay tacksman charged by Lord Reay with supervising the salmon river, the great deer preserve to the west, and the important black cattle pastures on Ben Hope. Rob Donn's way of life was typical of how people lived in the Reay country just before the collapse of the old order. His access to high and low in society gives the lie to apologists for the 'Improvements', that all was want and famine beforehand.

Either continue on to Alltnaharra (NC 569359) and follow the Strathnaver Trail along the B873 and B871 to Bettyhill or retrace your steps to the coast and rejoin the A838 to cross the Moine. This is a high, boggy moor. Always dangerous to cross, a metalled road, which forms the basis of the present route, was first built in 1830 by the orders of the incoming laird, the 2nd Marquis of Stafford. It is 10 miles east from Hope to Tongue across the modern causeway over the Kyle of Tongue. Taking the old road from Tongue, travel about one and a half miles south until you see a granite pillar (NC 586550), a memorial to the 19th century bard of the Clearances, Ewan Robertson, who died near here in a snow storm. His famous song, *Mo mhollachd aig na caoraich mhor* – 'My curses on the big sheep', dismisses the Duke of Sutherland in scathing terms. One phrase states:

> *Gu'm b'ann an Iutharn an robh an shail, Gu'm b'fhearr leam Iudas lamh rium.*
> Were I with you in Hell to meet, I'd sooner stand with Judas.

It is 12 miles on the A836 through Borgie forest from Tongue to Bettyhill, situated on the east bank of Torrisdale Bay at the mouth of the River Naver. The most notorious Clearances in the Highlands were enacted here in upper Strathnaver in 1814. They were not the first, because in 1803 a sheep farm lease in the upper strath was granted by the financially-strapped Sutherland estate management. Vast investment from the Leveson-Gower fortune soon prompted a dramatic increase in sheep farming and consequent clearances. Around 80 families from Strathnaver were removed in 1807, many being forced into existing settlements on the north side of the strath in one of the worst winters of recent memory. Complaints of overcrowding soon surfaced and criticism was voiced of the Sutherland policies.

One of the catalysts for more ruthlessly planned removals was

Patrick Sellar, Sutherland Estate's sub-factor employed in 1809. He gained new leases for sheep farms and ordered many Strathnaver barns and homes to be burned to the ground. He behaved with callous indifference to the predicament of the evicted people, who were removed to plots of heather near the north coast. This led to his sensational trial in Inverness in April 1816. Through the efforts of local people, Strathnaver Museum has been established at Clachan, Bettyhill in the old Farr parish church (NC 715622). The museum stands about 250 yards from the A836. It is about 30 miles west of Thurso, and is open from April to September with party bookings at other times by arrangement. This forms the last point on the recently marked-out Strathnaver Trail. Leaflets are available widely and include evidence of human habitation in the area from earlier times.

There are many pre-Clearance sites to be visited in the strath, and the Strathnaver Museum is a good starting point to understand the various phases of Clearance. Achanlochy (NC 716586) one and a half miles south of Naver Bridge on the minor road to Skelpick, was one of the last townships in the strath to be cleared. Follow the signs to the path; the base walls of houses, barns and kailyards are clearly visible. Dunviden (NC 726519) is a further two miles south of Skelpick, on a track to Rhifail. An ancient chambered tomb and a broch are to be found near house foundations of this cleared township; the remains of a corn kiln can also be seen.

Rosal is one of the largest townships to have been cleared, partly in 1814 and also four years later. This village, which contained homes for about 13 families, was excavated during the 1960s and artefacts are to be found in Strathnaver Museum. It is now on a well set-out trail with explanatory plaques. To walk to Rosal (NC 690415) start from the small car park three quarters of a mile south of Syre along a Forestry Commission track on the east bank of the Naver. There is a plaque (NC 684416) to Donald MacLeod, directly across from the site of Rosal, on the opposite bank of the River Naver south from Syre on the B873. Thirty years after the brutal events that he witnessed in Strathnaver, MacLeod wrote *Gloomy Memories,* which has gone through many editions to the present day. He was stung into response by the publication of *Sunny Memories* by Harriet

Beecher Stowe, author of *Uncle Tom's Cabin,* who was full of glowing praise for the Sutherland dukes.

Achadh an Eas was a settlement and graveyard (NC 666375) on the east side of Loch Naver, approximately one mile from the A837 and five miles south of Rosal. Grumbeg was a settlement and a graveyard (NC 635385) situated on the west side of Loch Naver, beside the A837, approximately six miles from Achadh an Eas and six miles from Altnaharra; it was cleared at the same time.

At Grummore, on the west side of Loch Naver (NC 606366) and on the west side of the A873, the foundations of houses and croft dykes are easily seen over an area of many acres. Patrick Sellar's house (NC 692438) is still inhabited; it is sited just west of the junction of the B873 and B871 at Syre and south of the more recent Syre Lodge. The dreary road south-east across heather moors and bog travels 33 miles via Kinbrace and down Kildonan Strath on the A897, back to Helmsdale. Alternatively, follow the Strathnaver Trail route north to Bettyhill.

Our north coast journey continues east on the A836 into Caithness to the west of Reay in a distance of 19 miles. Much is made of the sanctuary and work found in Caithness by the evicted natives of Sutherland. But a catalogue of later local Clearances was listed by witnesses at the Crofters' Commission hearing in Lybster Free Church on 4 October, 1883.

Take the minor road east from its junction with the A836 at the bridge over the Achvarasdale burn (NC 976650). Immediately ahead is the Hill of Shebster and at its foot another minor road leads south via the abandoned village of Broubster (ND 038596) to Shurrery Lodge (ND 038563) on the Forss Water. These lands were part of Sandside Estate in the 19th century. In 1838, 27 families were evicted from the former and 31 families from the latter. Five of the latter were offered wet ground holdings elsewhere and were allowed to break in the land.

Retracing your route to Reay continue east along the A836 and in the land dominated for the past 50 years by Dounreay nuclear test site. Evictions took place at Buldoo (NC 995671) and Achreamie (ND 015666) in the 1840s. It is documented that 67 families were evicted to make way for bigger farms around Dounreay (ND 000660), Skiall (ND 023673) and Borrowston (ND 016690). One crofter told Napier that the factor John Paterson had 'a few crofters kept as slaves'. In the whole area some 170 families were cleared between 1838 and 1860.

Twelve miles further along the A836 through Thurso to Castletown reaches another area of major land consolidation and evictions. The estate of the Earl of Caithness at Olrig (ND 185663), just south of Castletown, had no crofters by 1860 and on three other estates small tenants were rack-rented. Dunnet parish experienced major consolidation of farms from the 1840s onward. Take the B876 from Castletown and in another mile (ND 208668) a sign for Greenland indicates a minor road inland from Dunnet Bay. In this area West Greenland (ND 229674), Lochend (ND 265682) on Sinclair of Freswick's lands and Hollandmake (ND 263695) and Reaster (ND 260655) on those of Mr Traill of Rattar, dozens of families were put off their old tenancies. Witnesses described the harrowing scenes that led to temporary settlements graphically named Beggarstown and Pauperstown near the latter. From having few paupers before 1840 the parish had to support many families thereafter. It was also observed that the revolution in farming practice had not been all success as several big farmers were bankrupt by 1880, no doubt due to cheap foreign competition for their produce. In 1882 desperation forced poor tenants to break the wire fence around Hill of Dunnet (ND 195735) which protected the laird's grouse moor. They drove their starving stock onto the pasture available there.

Significant tenant agitation arose in the Land League era on the estate of Mains of Clyth (ND 280362) which lies 12 miles south of Wick on the A99. Tenant grievances came from a history of serial improvements and rack-renting. The Sinclairs of Ulbster held these lands up to 1863 and their tacksmen from 1788 to 1840 were members of the Henderson family. More sub-tenants meant more income and opportunities from the herring fishing were enticing. So they gave unbroken land on the Clyth Burn at Roster (ND 260400) to Sutherland crofters evicted from Tongue between 1802 and 1805 and from Kildonan in 1819.

Holdings were amalgamated without compensation for older houses and helped tenants build new homes with draining and ditching. The Sinclairs then continued reorganisation and removed 4,000 acres of common grazings to make sheep farms, raised rents for them and as a result several tenants left rather than pay any more rent. From 1863 to 1865 Adam Sharp, his descendants and their trustees owned Clyth. His rack-renting and demands for securities to back tenant arrears provoked more tenants to leave and raised communal demands for abatement through a petition to the proprietor and public debate in the local press. The story was told by crofters' representatives to be followed by noisy scenes that accompanied Mr Sharp's evidence to the Napier Commission. The result was 50 per cent reductions granted by the new Crofters' Commission in 1889.

Nine miles further south reaches Dunbeath (ND 160298) on the A9. In 1835 Sinclair of Freswick carried out a Clearance that provoked considerable unrest following a hard-hearted response from the landlord who deprived 107 families of pastures at Badfern, with

Badbea ruins and monument

no provision for alternative lots. Intercession by the local minister was of no avail.

Another notable Clearance site is reached on the A9, 10 miles further south. On the Ord of Caithness, at a lay-by there is a sign for a half mile path over the heather to Badbea (ND 089201). The village, now deserted, was built here on an inhospitable cliff-top site by people desperate for scraps of land. Those who landed there were evicted from Langwell in 1793. They were joined by some families from Ousdale and others evicted from Berriedale by Sir John Sinclair of Ulbster. Others joined them in 1830, having been evicted from Auchencraig by orders of the landlord Donald Horne. Donald Sutherland of New Zealand placed a monument and plaque. It remembers his father who emigrated in 1839. A story is also told of children and animals being tethered to stop them falling over the nearby cliffs. Many other Badbea settlers emigrated to North America and New Zealand; the last inhabitant left in 1911.

# CHAPTER 2

# Mainland Ross-shire

THERE WAS WIDESPREAD civil disobedience in Ross-shire in 1792, when the folk in the Easter Ross glens tried to drive the *caoraich mhor*, or great sheep, out of the county in 1792. Though they failed the landowners subsequently engineered the wholesale eviction of thousands from the fertile inland glens to the barren coasts, with the backing of the established church, for their free market approach. However in Coigach in 1852, and with the Bernera Riot in Lewis in 1874, there were some successful attempts to thwart landlord plans, following the famine years. By the 1880s fishing and farming crises spurred the small crofters and cottars to use their recently acquired political muscle through the Land League and the extension of the male franchise to tenants in the countryside. The example of Irish successes made a crucial difference.

Twelve miles west of Inverness the A862 reaches the Lovat Bridge (NH 517449). This was built to a Telford design in 1811 and is still – with some modifications – in use today. Two hundred and fifty yards upstream was the Stock Ford of Ross, the ancient crossing point on the River Beauly for livestock and soldiery. As the boundary of Ross and Inverness this was the destination for the abortive Strathrusdale sheep droving protest of 1792. Follow the main road one and a half miles north through Beauly to the junction with the B9169 signposted for Cromarty. Turn east after half a mile onto the A832, for five miles leading to Tore roundabout. The route drives through the lands of Kilcoy that were consolidated and broken in as arable ground by Clearance victims from surrounding estates that include people from Strathconon (see below).

This road runs through Killearnan. David Denoon, the minister of Killearnan Parish, was an early critic of the sweeping changes wrought by the Improvers. He wrote in the *Old Statistical Account* of 1792:

There is much evidence of the amalgamation from 20 to 60 acres, abolishing runrig, with proper leases given. . . the practice of uniting small farms makes it easier to collect rent for the proprietor, (making for) more rapid realisation of property's utmost value . . . two objections arise; for actual labour, the family was much more reliable husbandmen than hired servants. . . In the national view, the consolidation of farms is still more seriously objectionable. Its effect is immediate depopulation. It compels the aborigines to emigrate, friendless and unprotected, to other countries, or to crowd into towns with the view of grasping at the casual sources of earning their pittance that may occur.

Ill fares the land, to hastening ills a prey,
Where wealth accumulates, and men decay
Princes and lords may flourish, or may fade,
But a bold peasantry, their country's pride,
When once destroyed, can never be supplied.
 Oliver Goldsmith – The Deserted Village.

Were it possible to introduce the improvements of modern husbandry on farms of the above extent, just sufficient to occupy the attention, and encourage the exertions of the actual labourer aided by his family, that point would be achieved which would happily combine humanity with public utility and the real interest of the proprietors with the happiness of thousands of their fellow creatures.

Take the A835 (T) signposted for Ullapool and Dingwall for just over a mile to the signed minor road marked Drynie Park. There are fine views towards Strathconon to the west. Small crofts are laid out along the road for one and a half miles. Kenneth Davidson of Upper Knockbain, Kilcoy Estate gave evidence to the Napier Commission on Crofting 10 October 1883 describing how the drop in population in the previous 30 years related to evictions and removals from cottars and crofters who had first been given improving leases in the area then moved on again.

The factor's farm was once 21 crofts. Whenever the crofters have succeeded in reclaiming the land, they were evicted to make way for big farmers. We are, in short, made to reclaim the land for the proprietor, free of charge. At one time our forefathers possessed the undisputed rights to graze cattle on Mulbuie Common, which the landlords and clergymen have recently arrogated and divided among themselves. They have thus become the unjust owners of the land which was once common for the benefit of us and other poor people in the Black Isle. We demand an equivalent to what has been stolen from us. (RCC Edinburgh, HMSO, 1884, para. 40821)

Turn north-east along the B9169, drive one and a half miles to the junction with the A835 (T) and four miles on to Dingwall. The Ross-shire capital has an important livestock market that filled the areas around the parish church but has now moved to Humberston on the outskirts of town where the Highland Drover project is now based. Half a mile west on the A834, turn north just before the industrial estate on a minor road to Dochcarty. The Heights of Inchvannie (NH 497602) are part of a line of Clearance villages hacked out of the hillside – without the slightest help from the estates – in the wake of the Clearances of lower Strathpeffer around 1800. The Napier Commission was told in 1883 that crofters dare not shoot rabbits because, as sub-tenants without a lease, they were at the mercy of the ground officers. Good views are to be had from the minor road along the Heights which runs parallel to the A834 from Dingwall to Strathpeffer.

On 31 October 1987, a commemorative monument and garden were inaugurated in honour of Caithness writer Neil Gunn, a native of Dunbeath who lived for many years at Brae Farm. The monument at the Heights of Brae (NH 519610) consists of a boulder and slabs of Caithness stone decorated with symbols and quotes from his work. It is sited near the point where the novelist used to cross the township road on his walks from Brae Farm to gain inspiration for novels such as his Clearances epic, *Butcher's Broom*, and *The Serpent*, a tale of life in the new crofting communities for the removed people.

Strathconon lies 15 miles west of Dingwall, via the A835. Turn south at Moy Bridge on the A832 and after three quarters of a mile turn west through Marybank on a minor road. The Balfours, a very rich family of Lowland merchants, cleared this extensive glen in several stages in the 1840s. Its people were settled on the Black Isle in Killearnan and on the Gower Crofts at Knockfarrel (NH 507584), a township that was laid out by the factors of a daughter of the Earl of Cromartie who married the Sutherland heir, hence the Stafford-related name.

The son of the Clearance laird, AJ Balfour, became Secretary of State for Scotland in the critical period of the 1886 Crofters' Wars and later became British Tory Prime Minister. As a youngster, Balfour took part in the family's first visit to the glen in the year after the Clearances, for deer shooting. He was placed in the second coach, with the women, in order to deflect the violent abuse that was feared. All were reportedly surprised at the ingratiating welcome received from the tenants and estate workers! Around 500 people had been removed.

In modern times sheep have, in turn, been ousted by a Danish laird to promote deer shooting as its core activity. Returning via the minor road across the Curin hydro dam to Little Scatwell, skirt Loch Achilty and rejoin the A835 (T) and drive west through the vast Contin Parish whose minister the Rev. Charles Downie wrote in the *New Statistical Account* c.1840:

> sportsmen range the moor and mountains unmolested these days and the people are now utter strangers to such amusements, for where the game is not let to English sportsmen, it is very carefully preserved . . . a larger rent is now paid for the privilege of shooting alone than was paid 45 years ago for the right of pasturing.

Join the A832 just past Garve and take the A890 at Achnasheen. It is 41 miles from Contin to Lochcarron. This is also the rail route towards Kyle of Lochalsh from Dingwall. Near Glen Carron Lodge there are remnants of native Scots Pine woods (NH 060050), now fenced and conserved. The ravages of over-grazing have left under one per cent of Scotland covered in native woodlands. Glen Carron also has examples of the kind of blanket forestry where wind blow and stark fence lines show the inadequate defences they provided against deer, sheep and climate. More environmentally friendly and aesthetically pleasing approaches are now being adopted to grow commercial timber. A quarter of a mile east of the junction of the A890 and the A896 is the farm of New Kelso, the name pointing to the importance of Border shepherds in the agricultural life of the area since 1800.

Two and a half miles southwest lies Lochcarron Village. In 1882, the year of the Battle of the Braes, workmen on Lochcarron estate (NG 900400) won a court battle against their landlord, Dugald Stuart, who had failed to pay them. As an act of revenge, the landlord decided to evict the parents of the victorious workmen from Slumbay (NG 890385), but their neighbours rallied round and deforced the law officers attempting to serve the eviction notices. When the estate changed hands soon after, the new owner revoked the notices of eviction.

Continuing about six miles north on the A896 to Loch Kishorn at Tornapress (NG 838422), you take the spectacular unclassified road, including several hairpin bends, to mount the Bealach nam Ba (Pass of the Cattle). It reaches a height of 626 m on the 11 mile route to Applecross. This remote and formerly roadless peninsula faces Raasay and Skye across the Inner Sound. In 1790 Lord Applecross attracted the wrath of Robert Burns, Scotland's national bard. In his *Address of Beelzebub* – to the Earl of Breadalbane, President of the Highland Society, Burns berates chiefs for stopping their clansfolk from seeking a better life in North America. Written just after the War of Independence, it satirised a stance taken by many lairds, like MacKenzie of Applecross, who on one hand lauds old Highland customs, while on the other hand demands their tenantry do their bit in the Napoleonic war effort:

Faith you and Applecross were right
To keep the Highland hounds in sight;
I doubt na' they would bid nae better,
Than let them aince out our the water,
Then up among thae lakes and seas,
They'll make what rules and laws they please . . .

In the 1960s the road was opened between Applecross and Shieldaig but this improvement in the infrastructure failed to save the many townships like Lonbain (NG 687530); its street of ruins are easily seen from the tourist route. Also in Cuaig (NG 705576), Fearnmore (NG 723606), Fearnbeg (NG 736597), Arinacrinachd (NG 745583) and Kenmore (NG 757577), ruined houses abound. Few have benefited from the new road to live in the wildly remote scenery that supported so many people, even in the late 19th century, of whom Alexander Livingston, a merchant of Fearnabeg told the Napier Commission in 1886:

> Complaint for the North Coast, Applecross – No road, distance over 20 miles; people numbering about 400; three schools; children kept back for want of a road; petition late Lord Middleton and refuse road; postman running 12 miles off the road; service kept back with rivers and burns, want of road whatever. To this we humbly crave the commissioners to draw their attention. . . .'
> (RCC para. 29896)

Inland on the shore of Upper Loch Torridon lies Diabeg where, the laird David Darroch, unlike many sporting proprietors, permitted crofter settlement in the 1880s. The A896 winds 17 miles to Kinlochewe through Glen Torridon beneath the mountains of Ben Alligan, Liathach and Ben Eighe, their steeply terraced Torridonian sandstone striated by deep glaciation. Turning west along Loch Maree on the A832, it is 20 miles to Gairloch. This extensive parish escaped the worst Clearances; its population reached 5,186 in 1851. The MacKenzie lairds prided themselves on their fair treatment of the tenantry, who nevertheless suffered from the lack of land to meet the rising population. In 1882, Sir Kenneth MacKenzie of Gairloch owned 164,000 acres of Ross-shire. He accepted the appointment as one of the Napier Commissioners though he declined to sit at the Poolewe hearing on his own land. On his estate in 1843, at a time when legal trustees were operating, subdivision was carried out at North Erradale (NG 743810), where access to the common grazing was denied to crofters who were charged separately for lots of arable and common grazing. This was a similar pattern with other Highland estates, with landowners other lairds squeezing more rent out of tenants for smaller holdings. (RCC para 28884).

Journeying north on the A832 from Gairloch via Poolewe,

Aultbea and Laide, the traveller might well wonder how a greater population would fare in such a wild environment. However, advocates of sporting estates and 'last great wilderness' disciples are still suggesting that there is not enough land in the Highlands for more people. The radical land campaigner Andy Wightman noted that while the population of Wester Ross in some 550,000 acres stood at 4,000, only around 275 live more than a mile from the coast: no more than 300 people live in 536,000 acres of land.

Looking north from Laide you can see the bulk of Gruinard Island. Many have heard of it due to its deliberate contamination with anthrax in a chemical warfare experiment during World War Two. Few will know of the systematic removal of the resident population from the huge land area between the north shores of Loch Maree and the fertile coastal strip around Gruinard Bay. From the late 18th century the demands for cattle and sheep for city markets induced various branches of the MacKenzie family and also the Davidsons of Tulloch to sell parcel after parcel to incomers.

A Perthshire drover John Macintyre and his wealthy Yorkshire partner John Birtwhistle began by clearing Strath na Sealag and resettled the displaced people around the Gruinard. In 1803 James Hogg, known as the 'Ettrick Shepherd', was on his Highland tour to promote sheep farming. He saw standing crops abandoned by cleared small holders from that Strath.

This process continued throughout the 19th century and was particularly heartless under the orders of Lancashire coal owner Meyrick Bankes who owned the Gruinard Estate from 1835 and Letterewe from 1837. In almost every year from 1848 till 1871 he removed tenant family after family in search of a few pounds extra profit. Highlights of his actions included popular but ultimately futile resistance in 1860 and his removal in 1871 of some remaining people who had set up home in Polachan Cave (NB 913917) at 1st Coast. The remaining people were rescued by the Crofting Acts but landlord tyranny and opportunities elsewhere reduced the population of the whole of Gairloch Parish from 5,186 people in 1851 to 4,594 in 1881; the bulk of the losses being from Laide, Little Gruinard, 1st, 2nd and 3rd Coasts.

From the road high above the coast of Little Loch Broom you can cast an eye on Scoraig (NH 000962) on the north shore. Scoraig successfully resettled, and now has about one hundred inhabitants. It is 44 miles to the Braemore junction of the A832 with the A835 (T) to Ullapool. Before reaching Braemore, the route crosses the 'Destitution Road' in Dundonnell Forest (a mainly treeless preserve for deer and other game as with all deer forests). Following the great famine of 1846–48 the Board of Relief coordinated lairds in various parts of the north, in this case between Gairloch and Lochbroom. As Tom Atkinson wrote in *The Empty Lands*:

> There were no free lunches in those days, and to qualify for meagre handouts of meal, men had to put in a hard day's labour on the road. Women too received relief, but only if they produced a certain amount of spinning and knitting. Those who did not work hard enough received no meal. There were claims too that relief was often withheld from those who refused to give up their Catholic beliefs. The very old, the pregnant and the crippled were given special consideration. They only had to produce half the labour of the able-bodied, but then they received only half the rations anyway.

There are many such Destitution Roads in Scotland – see also the A838 Lairg to Loch Laxford road in Sutherland.

Around six miles north of Braemore is the road sign for the minor road to Letters, and the series of townships perched precariously on the north side of Loch Broom, all Clearance villages. Four miles further on the A838 lies Leckmelm (NH 170901). In 1879 the new owner, Aberdeen paper tycoon AC Pirie, instructed his factor that the tenants' grazings and plough lands were to be taken back by the estate, and that the tenants should be allowed to keep their cottages in return for work on the estates land. The local Free Church minister, Rev. John MacMillan, informed the press of these shameful changes. Widespread agitation was advocated by John Murdoch in his Inverness-based newspaper *The Highlander*. Such seeds of rebellion bore fruit only two years later at the Braes in Skye. The Rev. MacMillan assured the Crofters' Commission in 1883 that Pirie had been a kind employer; he also told of the loss of half of the population after 1879, as the young and fit left to seek work elsewhere. This shows how, 50 years after the large Clearances, landlord-power continued to put tenants in a precarious position.

Other surrounding areas had already been cleared: Inverlael in 1819–20, Strathnasheallag in 1803, Mungasdale in 1850, and Glackfour and Foich in 1842.

At Ullapool, a fishing port set up as a planned village in 1788, there is the ferry terminal for Stornoway on the Isle of Lewis. The award winning Ullapool Museum, West Argyle Street (Tel: 01854 612987), houses many relics of local life and lore. From Ullapool in 1773 one of the early emigrant parties sailed for Pictou in Nova Scotia aboard the sailing ship *Hector*. Commemorating their harrowing and brave story, a replica of the *Hector* was built as a millennium project in the Nova Scotia, Canada, keeping links to Loch Broom alive.

Twenty-five miles north-west of Ullapool is the peninsula of Coigach. Strath Kanaird, on the way to the Drumrunie road junction, experienced the emptying of houses in recent times by a laird whose policy was to keep many estate-owned houses empty. Beyond the miniature Assynt peak, Stac Polly 613 m, the narrow road reaches the coast at the crofting townships of Achnahaird, Polbain, Achiltibuie and Badenscallie. The Earl of Cromartie, who was able to find space in the east around Knockfarrel for evicted tenants from Strathconon, attempted rearrangements in his Barony of Coigach which met with repeated and eventually successful, popular resistance in 1853. 'Repulsed by the collective will of the rebellious tenantry', the scheme was dropped. Many factors in the north regarded this as 'spineless capitulation threatening all rights of property' (*The Scotsman*, 2 April 1853). A small, tenacious community mixes crofting, tourism and fishing to this day and Coigach's pipers, many of them young women, play tunes for village occasions with plenty wind to spare.

The main road the A894 runs eight miles north-east to Ledmore and then 11 miles south-east on the A837 to Strath Oykell. This isolated northern section of the old county of Ross was the scene of major Clearances instigated by Munro of Novar in 1820. Reach Culrain (NH 577948) by diverting from the A837

(NC 242125) signed to Doune and travelling six miles on a minor road. Militia led by Sheriff MacLeod, who had pursued the Strathrusdale sheep drovers in 1792, met a stone-throwing crowd incensed by the shooting of a woman by an over-eager militiaman. The sheriff and troops retreated in disarray to Ardgay Inn before the local minister, the Rev. MacBean warned the Strath Oykell people to render unto Caesar what was Caesar's, or risk the wrath of God! He was also angered by the treatment meted out to his parishioners and brought about a peaceful negotiation and subsequent removal, so that sheep farming tenants could move in. Novar made no provision for the out-going tenants.

Ten miles inland from Ardgay, west on minor roads along Strath Carron, is the scene of two major Clearances in 1845 and 1853. In 1816 Croick Church (NH 457914) was built to a design by Thomas Telford. The famous road and bridge builder also designed churches that were financed by parliament money in order to consolidate the Protestant religion in the Highlands. The Church of Scotland Disruption in 1843 left only two families and no minister remaining in the congregation at Croick, the other 18 families having seceded with the Rev. Gustavus Aird to the Free Kirk.

In 1843 the estate factor, Gillanders, set out to clear Glen Calvie two and a half miles south from Croick Church. Residents destroyed the writs of eviction, but they finally accepted compensation of £18 per holding. Of the 80 or so dispossessed Glen Calvie people the majority stayed in Croick churchyard for several nights after the evictions.

A reporter from the London *Times* investigating conditions in the north ahead of the passage of the new Poor Law for Scotland saw their lean-to shelters and recorded their story for posterity. Today we can read the pathetic messages scratched on the outside of the church's east window. Slogans such as 'Glencalvie people – the wicked generation' and 'Blowship me to the colonies' sum up their plight. Open all year, the church holds monthly summer services at Croick Church from May, the anniversary of the Glen Calvie evictions. While these evictions were being carried out, the absentee laird, Mr Robertson of Kindeace, was in Australia. The big house (NH 723733) can be

Croick Church near Glencalvie

found off the road between Tomich and Newmore parallel to the
A9 (T), four miles north-east of Invergordon, Easter Ross.

Greenyards (NH 520920) lies three miles east of Croick on the
south side of Strath Carron. Along the track here in 1853 there was
a bloody assault by police on the women of townships chosen for
eviction in one of the last Clearances in the area. Known as 'the
Massacre of the Rosses', it was reported by a Glasgow lawyer,
Donald Ross. Though he did not incite law breaking or resistance
to the Sheriff Officers, he acted as a major publicist of these events.
Two of the rioters, a man and a woman, were sentenced to 18 and
12 months hard labour respectively for breach of the peace. This
story was dramatised in John McGrath's ceilidh play, *The Cheviot,
the Stag and the Black Black Oil*.

Boath and Strathrusdale can be reached by following the A836
south-east from Ardgay for three miles then taking the B9176 via
the former Altnamain droving inn to Ardross. A cattle stance at
Stittenham, a reminder of the old livestock trade, was marked until
recently on OS maps; the name is another Stafford family import.

The drove stance was put under conifer forestry, now felled revealing the natural holding area for beasts en route for market. On minor roads, five miles north-west of Alness is the scene of the most southerly point reached by the Strathrusdale men in their attempt to drive all the sheep out of the county in 1792. Leave the A836 Struie road at Contullich (NH 639704). The great sheep drive which started on the banks of the Oykell, took the hill pass from Strath Carron via Glen Calvie or the route up the Wester Fearn Burn via Garvary (NH 597862) which figures in a song about illicit whisky distilling. High-handed actions of incoming sheep tenants, who impounded the straying cattle, owned by local residents, prompted a huge drive of around 20,000 sheep south to Boath (NH 570740). The 'drovers' dispersed when troops of the Black Watch were sent to aid the landlords. Little remains of the settlements which produced this early resistance to the replacement of people by sheep.

From the road to Boath, the blades of modern windmills can be seen glinting in the sun, on towers that top the hills behind the township. Ardross Castle, built by Alexander Matheson in the 1840s is to the north across the strath. Matheson had increased the number of holdings in the area to create more small farms unlike his policy on the west coast in Kintail. Beyond Novar Toll take the B817 along the loop road to Evanton. You pass by the mansion on Novar estate from which the major Clearances at Strath Oykell were planned. The much-reduced Novar estate still boasts 20,000 acres of farming, forestry and shooting lands. On Cnoc Fyrish (NH 668698) is the largest of three follies built c.1795 by Sir Hector Munro, the construction of which is said to have given work to landless labourers; no doubt evicted through his estate Improvements. It represents the gates of Nangapotam, an Indian city sacked by Munro's regiments. A tourist in 1829 was not impressed:

> From the Bridge of Alness, where we had reposed on the previous night, we enjoyed a fine view of the fir-clad hills above Novar, crowned by a Gothic screen, more nearly resembling a gigantic brotherhood linked hand in hand, than the dilapidated remains of any fabric whatsoever. Indeed it is difficult to conjecture the

motive which could induce any man to make bad taste so con-
spicuous, as in these imitative antiquities. (B Botfield, *Tour of the
Highlands*)

Taking the minor road marked Swordale in the middle of Evanton
you reach a dead end after three miles, with views into Glen Skiach.
Major Jackson, a wealthy Dundee industrialist, bought the Swordale
estate in the 1880s with vacant possession, i.e. the seller, Mr Munro,
agreed to remove all sitting tenants. This was achieved in stages in
the late 1870s when the lease on Swordale Farm itself was resumed
and the five tenant crofters and their shepherd were evicted from
Clare (NH 543652), West Clare and Strath Skiach. Jackson sought
to employ all the dispossessed as farm servants and ghillies. His
philanthropy included the building of the Diamond Jubilee Hall in
Evanton, where his full size portrait adorns the stage. In consequence of the removal of tenants from Swordale, Jackson arranged
for the carving out of allotments for villagers to grow vegetables.
Evanton like many other Highland villages grew from the emptying
of the countryside.

Arguments for resettlement of upland straths such as Strath
Skiach were addressed to the Royal Commission on Deer Forests
in Scotland when it took evidence in 1892. However, plans for the
resumption of a million acres of deer forest for land settlement were
only achieved in very small part in the following 30 years. Strath
Skiach was included, but never returned to crofting. Clare has been
under blanket forestry since the 1960s, the remains of 5,000 years of
human settlement swamped by serried ranks of conifers.

In commemoration of the bi-centenary of the birth of stone
mason and journalist Hugh Miller, a slab of Caithness stone has
been erected at his native Cromarty, the small port at the mouth of
the Cromarty Firth. Many emigrants sailed from there to the New
World and one such party in 1831 leaving on the ship *Cleopatra*
was witnessed by Miller. The monument on the foreshore at
Cromarty (NH 788678) can be reached in 17 miles along the B9163
from south of the Cromarty Bridge on the A9.

# CHAPTER 3

# Strath Glass, Glen Moriston, Glenelg and Kintail

THE MacDONNELLS OF GLENGARRY, the Chisholms of Strath Glass, the Clanranald MacDonalds and the Seaforth MacKenzies disposed of their 'surplus' population with appalling rapacity.

Abriachan is a small community (NH 557353) high above Loch Ness, about seven miles south-west of Inverness. It is reached by a minor road branching west from the A82 on a loop from (NH 624417) south of Dunain; it is signposted for Caplich. This area has an unbroken tradition of small farms and crofting and benefited from the decision of the Speyside-based Seafield estate not to clear their small tenantry, unlike the surrounding estates. Abriachan life in the 20th century has been chronicled by Katharine Stewart in *Abriachan: The Story of an Upland Community* to celebrate the recent purchase of local forestry for community use.

Take the minor road north-west from Abriachan (NH 354557) through Glen Convinth, crossing the A833 to Kiltarlity. Continue half a mile west on the minor road to the junction a mile and a half north to Kilmorack, catching a glimpse on the way of Beaufort Castle, the home of the Lovat Frasers for centuries until the death duties and the poor balance of family finances forced its sale in the late 1990s. The old parish church of Kiltarlity and Convinth lies less than a mile apart across the River Glass from the old parish church of Kilmorack (NH 494444). They are now much closer due to the bridge and hydro dam developments. This is the heart of the Lovat lands that were managed so as to create sheep farms and deer forests in the extensive glens running west. The parish, which extends over 35 miles west to the headwaters of Glen Affric, was shared till the early 19th century with the extensive estates of the chiefs of the Chisholm clan whose seat was at Erchless Castle in Strath Glass.

The small deer forest of Urchany and Farley can be viewed from township roads signposted for Torgormack and Farley, half a mile west of Kilmorack church. Urchany was never cleared as such, but the ancient population gradually abandoned higher ground as sheep grazing gave way to deer forest use.

Monar Forest west of Glen Strath Farrar was cleared in 1792, with farms and lots elsewhere being offered to those families removed. Enter the glen six miles south-west of Kilmorack church on the A831 at the junction (NH 402414). Permission to drive west has to be obtained at the gate house purportedly to protect the wildlife of the area by restricting the number of cars that enter. Not only did sheep farming thin out the communities in these far flung glens, but the subsequent creation of deer forests in the 19th century saw sheep stocks sold off and the only employment available being for keepers and deer watchers.

The heirs of The Chisholm, the ancient chief of Glen Cannich, conducted extensive Clearances for sheep farming, tripling rents from 1787 to 1792. From 1801 onwards, in both Kiltarlity and Kilmorack parishes, hundreds of families were removed until there was hardly a tenant of their name. One of the evicted, Donald Chisholm, blacksmith of Glen Affric composed a bardic lament. 'Our chief is losing his kin! He prefers sheep in his glens, and his young men in the camp of the Army!'

When you drive through the strath and its feeder glens the variety of scenery and excellent land for both arable and pasture suggest that a far greater population might still live there profitably. The emigration of many Kilmorack people in 1801 on board the *Dove of Aberdeen* and the *Sarah of Liverpool*, which both took aboard far too many passengers, was used as an example of why emigration should be staunched, and led to the Passenger Act of 1803. An agent, George Denoon, had set up a trading post at Pictou, Nova Scotia, and needed customers for his store. The passenger lists include many Chisholms from the parish whose occupation was listed as 'late farmer'. Conditions were dreadful and many died on the prolonged voyage. The lairds' arguments for stopping emigration on humanitarian grounds ring hollow – this was the age of the press gang and they wanted manpower for the wars with Napoleon! The Act was repealed in 1827, by which time the lairds were arguing that the Highlands were over-populated.

From Cannich (NH 338318) there is a choice of routes. Either walk through Glen Affric by the old coffin road to Kintail, or over the old droving route that took the cattle and sheep south from Tomich in Glen Cannich over to Torgyle in Glen Moriston. Alternatively, drive on the A831 via Glen Urquhart to Loch Ness-side and south-west to Invermoriston on the A82 (T), some 25 miles. Travelling west on the A887 another 37 miles takes you to Shiel Bridge (NG 935188) in Kintail. In Glen Shiel there is the site of the battle where Jacobites, backed by Spanish troops, were defeated in 1719.

Of the emptying of these glens to make way for sheep farms, the Rev. Morrison of Kintail wrote in 1845, that 'rents were raised, the people became poor, they were either deprived of, or voluntarily gave up, their possessions; and many, who then, were in good circumstances . . . now live in penury' (NSA parish of Kintail, Ross-shire).

There are two possible routes to the Isle of Skye. To drive via Dornie on the A87 to Kyle of Lochalsh, or to take a detour to Plockton at Auchtertyre on the A890 driving six miles north to Achmore and then five and a half miles west, by a very narrow road past the vast Victorian pile of Duncraig Castle (NG 814333), best seen from Plockton village. Alexander Matheson was a nephew of James Matheson who bought Lewis in 1845. Both made a fortune from the family firm, Jardine Matheson. Alexander claimed to have left before the trade in opium boosted the company balances. He applied his fortune both at Ardross and on his sporting property in Kintail. He told the Napier Commission at Balmacara in 1883, in an outburst from the floor, that he could well do with half of his remaining tenants to emigrate.

The view opens up across the Inner Sound to Raasay and the Cuillins of Skye; at Drumbuie crofting communities still cultivate the reasonably flat, fertile strips.

Eight and a half miles west from Shiel Bridge over Mam Ratagan and down Glen More, the road follows the old military road to Glenelg. This fertile corner of Lochalsh was emptied of people early in the 19th century when the inhabitants of Glen Beg and Glen More were first moved into overcrowded townships on the shores of the Sound of Sleat. The MacLeod lands thereabouts had been sold in 1810 to pay off family debts; like most Highland estates of the period the estate was bought by sportsmen and rich industrialists from elsewhere. Glenelg was badly hit by the failure of the potato crop in 1847; an English visitor described the homes of the people as, 'wretched, filthy, smokey, unglazed and in every respect comfortless hovels. . .'

The Iron Age brochs in Glen Beg show the value placed on these fertile pockets of land through thousands of years, while the shell of Bernera Barracks (NG 815197) at Glenelg was a stronghold of the Hanoverian military, used to protect the main route to the west coast. There is a ferry to Kylerhea over the sea to Skye in the summer months across the narrows where cattle were swum across the tide race, en route for southern cattle trysts in the 18th and early 19th centuries.

# CHAPTER 4

# Skye and Raasay

ISLANDS OFTEN FORM a microcosm of a region: Skye is one such, with historical associations with the earliest Celtic people, the ruinous 1745 Rebellion with its multiple evictions that followed and with the crofters' fight back in the 1880s. The starkly beautiful scenery of the winged island has long attracted visitors whose recollections, combined with the long memories of its native people, have handed down a treasury of love. The experience of the island's people at the hands of their landlords, the MacLeods and the MacDonalds, was no better than elsewhere in the Highlands.

On their Highland journey Dr Johnson and his companion James Boswell saw many symptoms of change in the Highlands. Take the road from Kylerhea to the Scullamus junction of the A850 and then some 16 miles south on the A851 to reach Armadale where Johnson and Boswell stayed in Sleat with Sir Alexander MacDonald in October 1773. Boswell recounted:

> we performed with much activity a dance which I suppose the emigration from Skye has occasioned. They call it 'America'. A brisk reel is played. The first couple begin, and each sets to one – then each to another – then as they set to the next couple, the second and third couples are setting; and so it goes on until all are set a-going, setting and wheeling round each other, while each is making the tour of all in the dance. It shows how emigration catches till all are afloat. Mrs MacKinnon told me that last year when the ship sailed from Portree for America, the people on shore were almost distracted when they saw their relations go off; they lay down on the ground and tumbled, and tore the grass with their teeth. This year there was not a tear shed. The people on shore seemed to think that they would soon follow. This is a mortal sign.

The *Christian Watt Papers* provide a remarkable insight into the west coast scene through the acute eye of an independently-minded, fisher-wife from Broadsea, Fraserburgh. Many Buchan girls followed the herring boats to gut fish in the 1840s. Christian's recollections include a scathing indictment of the recent Skye Clearances and harsh treatment of the people by Lord MacDonald. After an attempt by his factor to 'remove' a girl's barrels of gutted herring, Christian confronted the laird at Kyleakin quay. 'You are lower than the outscourings of a pigsty, causing all that suffering to innocent people,' she told him, adding:

> Had he been on the east coast, his fine castle would have been burnt down; though I was a herring gutter I was as much a descendent of the Lord of the Isles as he was. We went to Lewis and Barra and Strathy in Sutherland. I liked travelling the fishing, for it gave a true picture of the Highland way of life, and the Clearances that the government turned a blind eye to.

Drive eight miles from Kyleakin along the A850 to Broadford and six miles west on the B8083 that continues to Elgol at the mouth of Loch Slapin, then take the rough track three miles south from Torrin. This reaches the abandoned township of Suishnish (NG 591160) and, in another mile or so, Boreraig (NG 622166). These were the scenes of a well-documented Clearance in 1854 by orders of MacDonald of Sleat. The Suishnish ruins lie on relatively fertile ground and the removals were witnessed by the eminent geologist Sir Archibald Geikie, who described the tragic scenes of tearful trudging families, in his *Scottish Reminiscences*, published in 1904. Many of the people subsequently emigrated to Australia but others were moved to Isle Ornsay, Drumfearn and Tarskavaig in Sleat and near Breakish in Strath. Much hardship was caused to the people, some of them are said to have settled on crofts on Skye's east coast at Strollamus (NG 590270), on the rocky slopes three miles north of Broadford on the A850. These were poor crofts in comparison to Suishnish. Nevertheless, they were clung to by several generations. As recently as 1972 a crofting demonstration was mounted there against a new, high-handed landlord, retired paper technologist, the late Horace Martin. Since his death and the accession of his son the estate has descended into a web of offshore ownership. Crofters do not know to whom they pay their rent. The development of the land is stalled.

Another six miles north along the A850 through steep passes on the edge of the Red Cuillins, lies Sconser, the port for Raasay. (Details for ferries to Raasay can be obtained from CalMac.) The island of Raasay lies one mile east of Skye. It is overlooked by the Braes, the site of earlier Clearances on Skye, where Sorley MacLean, the greatest Gaelic poet of the 20th century, lived and found inspiration. Hallaig (NG 590384) on the east coast of Raasay and nearby South Fearns show many ruins of homesteads. In the mid-19th century Raasay changed hands four times in 16 years, losing people at every change of laird. Its population has declined to one hundred or so. Much distress was caused by the obstructive policy of an absentee landowner in the 1970s, Dr Green, who was sold parts of the island by the Department of Agriculture and Fisheries who then paid him inflated prices for sell-ing back land for the new pier and Raasay House.

The crofts of Braes half a mile across Loch Sligachan can be seen from Sconser, but the main road first clings to the coast via Sligachan then crosses over the moors down to Portree, skirting Ben Lee along Glen Varigill. It is 17 miles to the junction with the B883 for the Braes. This historic series of townships, strung out eight and a half miles south to Peinchorran, was pitch-forked into the news in the 1880s by the desperation of its crofters who had driven their cattle illegally onto nearby Ben Lee. They deforced the sheriff offi-cers and the County Sheriff, his officers and 50 Glasgow Bobbies, imported for the occasion arrested their ringleaders. A memorial plaque in both Gaelic and English was unveiled in 1980 beside the cliff road where the melee was fiercest, just north of Gedintailor (NG 523356). In the 1880s the press called it the 'Battle of the Braes' and the start of the Crofters' War. The Napier Commission's first meeting to take evidence on 8 May 1883, was held in the Upper Ollach School, half a mile away.

Return to Sligachan and turn west on the A863, driving 24 miles to Dunvegan. Near Drynoch roadend (NG 412309) extensive strips of former cultivation on the steep slopes of Glendrynoch can be seen. The branch road B8099 leads to Talisker Distillery, Portnalong and the heart of the Cuillins in the district of Minginish. The A863 snakes north-west round picturesque Loch Bracadale, from which area Skye people were sold into white slavery in the 18th century North American colonies. With the connivance of the MacDonald and MacLeod chiefs a roundup of undesirables was loosely drawn by an unscrupulous tacksman, Norman MacLeod of Bernera, and a Donaghadee skipper William Davison. However their money-making plan came unstuck when some of the kidnapped Skye and Harris people escaped. Some returned to tell the tale and the plans were widely condemned. It was a foretaste of the collapse of clan loyalty, and the bonds between chiefs and clanspeople.

The MacLeods of Dunvegan hold 30,600 acres of Skye today. This includes much of the Black Cuillin Hills. In the 18th century the MacLeods owned more than double that area. From their castle (NG 247490) near Dunvegan a major Clearances programme was invoked in the early 19th century. Bracadale Parish, despite increased life expectancy, declined from 2,250 souls in 1795 to 1,769 at the 1831 census. The local minister, writing in 1845, blamed the growth of large sheep farms while the annual export of sheep eclipsed that of black cattle – 4,000 of the former to 450 of the latter. Many people applied for assisted passage to Canada in 1826 as more and more arable land in Bracadale and Duirinish was turned over to pasture, with more families being removed to Glendale. This stoked the resentment and land hunger that made the area a major centre of rebellion in the 1880s.

Colbost Blackhouse Museum (NG 216488) lies four miles west of Dunvegan on the B884. Set below Colbost Hill on the south side of Loch Dunvegan, it was the point from which the naval assault force sent to arrest the Glendale crofters in 1882, was first observed. The reconstructed blackhouse contains implements and furniture of bygone days, a peat fire burns in the middle of the floor and to one side you see a box bed. The museum is open daily, including Sundays, during the summer months. The award winning Three Chimneys Restaurant is nearby.

The Glendale Land League Monument (NG 198496) sits one and a half miles west on the B884 at Cnoc an t' Sithean on the pass that leads to Glendale. Funds collected in the 1920s after the death of Land League leader, John MacPherson, The Glendale Martyr, were finally used to build the memorial in 1970, on the site of a confrontation in 1882 between 500 crofters and a party of marines who were attempting to arrest the crofters' leaders. Stock had been driven illegally onto the land near Waterstein Head (NG 146471). The Napier Commission heard evidence in the Free Church (NG 176496) one and a half miles further on in the cluster of buildings at the mouth of the glen. The whole population of Duirinish became involved. The congested population had to cope not only with being limited in their land use to very restricted holdings but also with estate rules such as a ban preventing them from keeping dogs! The MacPherson MacLeod estate was bought by a Tory government in 1905 and sold to its tenants on 50-year mortgages. This failed to save the area from decay and depopulation.

Near the road junction of the minor road for Waterstein from Upper Milovaig (NG 155494) there is an obvious example of the old field system of runrigs, or *feannagan*. They characterise the people's need to cultivate every possible scrap of land to support life in such overcrowded pockets.

Lorgill is a cleared township (NG 178419) that can be reached by walking from Ramasaig. Drive 300 yards in the direction of Milovaig on the B884 miles from the Primary School at Hamaramore (NG 166494) and take the minor road three miles south to Ramasaig. Then you walk two miles by a rough track south-east of Ramasaig road end to the sheltered green sward of Lorgill where 10 resident families were given a month's notice and cleared in May 1830. The house sites and cropped grass around the in-bye land are a hint of past human endeavour. From Lorgill, all the way to the stacks of MacLeod's Maidens off Idrigill Point, the wild cliff-bound coast abounds in huge waterfalls, natural arches and caves. It is cut by a series of short, steep glens in which townships of islanders were systematically cleared in the 1820s to make way for sheep. Each glen is accessible on foot and best approached from Orbost.

From the junction at Lonmore (NG 267465) on the A863, take the B884 for three quarters of a mile to the sign for Orbost. The minor road winds two miles south past Orbost House where you reach the black basalt sand on the beach at Loch Bharcasaig. From here a rough track and hill path allows access four miles south to Idrigill (NG 250380). Via forested Glen Bharcasaig rough paths lead three miles over the bealach at a height of 250 m to Ollisdal (NG 215395) and (NG 205400). Each is another two miles downhill. According to Malcolm MacAskill, a 36 year-old crofter from Kilmuir, in evidence given to the Napier Commission in May 1883 at Dunvegan; Lorgill, Ramasaig, Ollisdal, Dibidal, Idrigill, Forse and Bharcasaig were systematically cleared. MacAskill's father was removed from each of the first four places in the process and the latter had seen Ramasaig and Lorgill depopulated twice (RC para.3901). MacAskill gave a full description of the oppression and overcrowding faced by the communities in graphic detail.

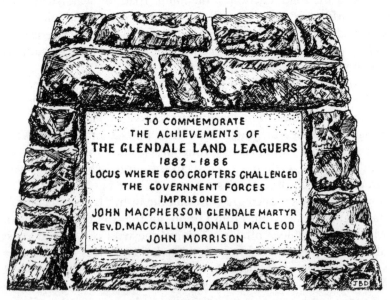

Glendale Land League monument

Orbost estate contains the last five of the above list of cleared townships. In 1997 its several thousand acres, which had been a working farm, were purchased by Skye and Lochalsh Enterprise for the price of £500,000 as an experiment in repopulation. Its future occupancy by modern Skye residents has had a troubled passage that is scarred by local scepticism concerning the agency's plans. All are agreed that more land, for housing and appropriate businesses, is required by the growing Skye population today and ironically echoes the pleas of the Kilmuir crofters in 1883.

Many parts of Skye experienced Clearances and the resistance to them. Take the A850 from Dunvegan to Portree – in three and a half miles the road passes by the old Fairy Bridge, the scene of the Land League meetings at which Mairi Mhor nan Oran, 'Big Mary of the Songs', roused the crofters to action. After another 14 and a half miles you pass by Lochs Greshornish and Snizort and the estate of Skeabost from which Mairi Mhor came.

Travelling round on the Trotternish peninsula north of Kensalyre on the A856 you pass by Kingsburgh (NG 395552); from here Allan MacDonald and his wife Flora travelled to America with their family and servants in 1773; later returning, having backed the losing Hanoverians in the American War of Independence. Flora is famous for helping to save Prince Charles Edward Stewart in 1746 when she guided him, in disguise as her maid, from South Uist to Skye. Her grave is to be found in Kilmuir Cemetery (NG 400718). The road then passes the port of Uig, where the ferry departs for North Uist and Harris, and after another five miles reaches the Kilmuir estate. Captain William Fraser from Nairnshire bought the Kilmuir estate from Lord MacDonald in 1855. He proceeded to rack-rent the crofters who responded with rent strikes, deforcement of the police squad billeted there and 'direct action' against estate property and livestock. Marines were landed in the winter of 1884; rents were reduced in the militant townships of Valtos (NG 514638) and Ellishader (NG 502655). The 45,337 acres of Kilmuir were bought by the government for £80,000 in 1904 and its crofters became tenants of the Secretary of State for Scotland, and now under the Scottish government's Environment and Rural Development Minister.

The government stationed troops and marines on Skye and in other trouble spots in the Western Isles, in the year following November 1884, in response to the Irish Land League tactics now being practiced by the 15,000 strong Highland Land League. The League won a major victory in the shape of the 1886 Crofters' Act giving fair rents, fixity of tenure and compensation for improvements for families with a crofting lease. However the cottars, or landless labourers, were given no redress.

# CHAPTER 5

# Harris and Lewis

A CALMAC FERRY sails from Uig to Lochmaddy in North Uist and also to Tarbert and Harris on the Outer Isles on a triangular route. In the early 17th century King James VI of Scotland and I of England attempted to repeat on the Outer Hebrides his earlier plantation of Ulster in order to reduce the power of the clan chiefs and to undermine the Gaelic culture of the people. Outside forces have shaped the land use of the Outer Isles thereafter. The cash-strapped Seaforth MacKenzies began Clearances in Lewis in the 1780s. The population explosion after the introduction of the potato in the 1740s put great pressure on available land. The Mathesons who owned Lewis and the Gordon Cathcarts, who owned South Uist and Barra, set about thinning out the population, from the Butt of Lewis to Barra Head.

The people were moved onto such small patches of land, scratching a bare subsistence by gathering kelp for the laird. The collapse of the kelp market in 1815 meant that a large number of people were effectively trapped on an area of land too limited to afford a proper livelihood if worked in the old communal manner. Not until 1920, after widespread land raids did some land resettlement take place in favour of the people, through government intervention.

At Tarbert (NG 157998), Isle of Harris, the settlement huddled around the pier is one result of past social engineering. Communities around the fertile shores of West Loch Tarbert and the Sound of Taransay were systematically cleared from the late 18th century onwards. Sir Alexander MacLeod had bought Harris in 1778 and developed the fishing; the island's population doubled in the next 50 years. In the 1820s major Clearances began along the west coast, specifically aimed to create huge sheep farms. Just as Sutherland sub-factor Patrick Sellar had been in pole position to bid for sheep farm lets on the land he factored, so were the factors of MacLeod

and Seaforth. Evictions and resettlements in rocky east Harris continued under the Earl of Dunmore's ownership from the mid-1830s
from his castle at Amhuinnsuidhe (NB 042082). To see today's remnants of the resettlement communities, travel on the A859 for four
and a half miles south from Tarbert take the minor road from
Drinnishadder via Manish and Finsbay, 12 and a half twisting
miles to Rodel (NG 048832). Looking at these patches of ground,
you can only marvel at the labour needed to survive from them and
be aghast at the term 'lazybeds' applied by some commentators.
The new settlers, used to relatively fertile pastures in the west of the
island, even remonstrated that there was not enough earth to bury
their dead! Needless to say, hundreds people took Dunmore's offer of
an assisted passage to Canada in the early 1840s. Another large
group sailed to Australia after the potato blight years, in 1854.

The woes of those remaining were catalogued graphically 30 years
later by Rev. Alexander Davidson, a Free Church minister in Harris,
in front of the Napier Commission:

> I would suggest that the people should get a competent portion
> of the earth to cultivate. The want of a road through the East
> Bays of Harris, and bridges on the rivers, is an unspeakable griev-
> ance and hardship. All the crofters pay road money. . . It is most
> unnatural that man should be chased away to make room for
> sheep and deer; that the land should lie uncultivated when men
> are perishing for lack of food. It is very unnatural that old or
> young should not be allowed to cast a hook into a standing lake
> or stream to catch a trout without being pursued by an officer of
> the law. . . (RC para.12992)

It is 21 miles through the wild mountain passes of North Harris,
and alongside Loch Seaforth on the A859 into Lewis to reach the
township of Balallan (NB 287207) some 15 miles south of the
island's capital, Stornoway. Balallan School was central to the
Pairc Deer Raid of 1887.

Lewis is on the northern portion of the largest island of the Western
Isles, sometimes known as the Long Island. It first experienced
Clearances as early as 1780 in the last decades of the MacKenzie

of Seaforth's ownership. People were forced to leave Barvas, Lochs, Uig, Stornoway and Park. Between 1780 and 1813 over 500 people were moved out to make way for sheep farming. The biggest Clearance was from Uig, in the west of Lewis, where wintering grounds and moor grazings were taken from the people. Between 1825 and 1828 some resettled on the west of the island at Brenish but many more left for Canada.

Those who were left on the island continued to be haunted by the cries of their families who had been forced to leave. Rack renting, kain, i.e. payment in kind for work on the estate, and 'road money' payments added to the people's grievances. Township after township was abandoned. Some Uig people were crowded into Ness (to reach Ness, follow the A857 for 28 miles north-west of Stornoway) where the museum opened by the local Heritage Society tells their story and much else of interest in local life and lore.

The diary of the Matheson factor, John Munro MacKenzie, details the plans to clear many Lewis townships that culminated in the removal of 400 people onto the emigrant ship that left Bernera on 19 May 1851. Over 20 years later the report of the Bernera Crofters' riot in 1874 by the *Highlander* newspaper was influential in inspiring crofters to get organised in the 1882 crisis.

In November 1887, the celebrated Deer Raid took place at Pairc. Local men led by Balallan schoolmaster Donald MacRae invaded the prohibited area and shot many deer in order to fed their starving families. MacRae was dubbed the 'Alness Martyr', because the previous year he had been sacked by the Rosskeen School Board in Easter Ross for being a Land League activist. He led and planned the raid on the nearby 32,000 acre deer forest from which starving, landless people were excluded. The leaders, including MacRae, who gave themselves up to the authorities, were charged with mobbing and rioting and found not guilty in a sensational trial in Edinburgh. A monument designed by Will MacLean was erected in 1995. In the form of a tower with doors leading to views of the main sites associated with the raid, it sits on a rocky mound at the entrance to the Pairc peninsula, looking like a Pictish tower of old.

A riot occurred in January 1888 when troops arrested would-be land raiders at Aignish Farm (NB 483324), where a cairn has now been erected. This can be reached four miles east of Stronoway on the A866, at the entry to the Eye peninsula.

Following the confrontation of crofters and cottars with Lord Leverhulme after World War One, the clash of cultures and ideas came to a head at Gress Bridge (NB 490412), which lies six miles north of Stornoway. Take the A857 and turn east on the B895 at Newmarket. Here stands another monument designed by Will MacLean, this time representing the complex meeting of Lord Leverhulme with the protesting cottars. Drastic civil disobedience was used to highlight the plight of the landless labourers who had been ignored by the 1886 Crofters' Act. These events led to widespread land redistribution during the following three decades. But Lewis had various upheavals to cope with, not least from Matheson's successor, the intransigent Lord Leverhulme, whose ambitious industrial plans had no place for crofting around Stornoway.

# CHAPTER 6

# Inverness, Strathnairn, Lochaber, Morvern, Mull and Moidart

INVERNESS TOLBOOTH, old courthouse and jail (NH 666453) was built in 1789, a symbol for the huge county of the town's modernity. The courthouse was scene of the trial of Patrick Sellar in April 1816. Robert McKid, the Sheriff Substitute for Sutherland, charged Patrick Sellar with culpable homicide, but he was acquitted by a jury of his peers on the direction of the judge, Lord Pitmilly. McKid was dismissed from office and ruined. In 1993, Highland Heritage raised a plaque on the tolbooth steeple's Church Street elevation to commemorate this famous miscarriage of justice. The plaque makes a plea in Gaelic for truth and justice to prevail, 200 years after the event. It reads:

> Patrick Sellar. In this place, the infamous Patrick Sellar was acquitted by a jury of his peers in April 1816, but he stands guilty in the memory of the Highland people. Sheriff Substitute Robert McKid who charged him with culpable homicide, fire raising and cruelty in the 1814 Strathnaver Clearances, was disgraced by the establishment. SE FIRINN IS CEARTAS A SHEASAS.'

Routes down the Great Glen on the east side of Loch Ness follow General Wade's military roads via Dores and Foyers via Strath Errick to Fort Augustus, or as an alternative off the A9 (T) onto the B851, in Strathnairn from Daviot driving 11 miles south-west to Crochy (NH 604243). About 400 m to the right of the drive to Dunmaglass Lodge, there is a pile of rocks 10 m in diameter. This was the site of a former township. At the age of 26, the last MacGillivray chief,

John William XIII, sold Dunmaglass to an Englishman, Colonel Sopper, in 1890. Some years later the Colonel had an altercation with a tenant whom he regarded as having been impudent. The tenant was given notice to quit, and when other tenants objected, all were evicted. Their homes were demolished and the house stones piled high in one great heap, presumably so that they could not return and the field used again. This mound of stones is a dramatic reminder of all the finality of such Clearances. The foundations of the township buildings are clearly visible around the rock pile.

A mile west from Crochy the B851 joins the B862 and follows the old route of the military road for some 15 miles to Fort Augustus. In Boleskine and Abertarff the parish minister noted a loss of 267 persons, or 13 per cent of the residents, in the ten years from 1821 to 1831, and noted that by 1845 there were 30,000 Cheviot sheep in the area.

Kilmonivaig is an extensive parish that straddles the Great Glen, including Glen Garry to the west and Glen Spean to the east. By the 1830s, 100,000 sheep were grazed in its glens with consequent

Stone pile of former village Dunmaglass

loss of homes and land for small farmers. In the 18th century the MacDonnell chiefs of Glen Garry adopted an extravagant lifestyle far beyond their means. No longer did 1,000 fighting men denote a chief's standing, his £300 rental would have to be increased one-hundred fold to meet debts. As early as the 1750s the MacDonnells were removing tenants from Knoydart to create sheep farms. The arrival in 1782 of Thomas Gillespie, an incoming sheepman, led to round after round of Clearances. You can look into Glen Quoich five miles west on the A87 road from Invergarry. High above Loch Garry from a roadside viewpoint at (NH 212028) you see in the now flooded glen the outline of a map of Scotland. For thousands of visitors from North America the flood took their names abroad.

Five hundred clanspeople were evicted from Glen Quoich in 1785. They sailed for Canada in terrible conditions aboard the ship *MacDonald* hoping to find relatives already planted in Glengarry, Quebec. Further Clearances from the western glens in 1785, 1787 and 1788 failed to balance the books. The old laird's death led to the inheritance of Alasdair Ranaldson MacDonnell, a bizarre figure who re-invented ancient clan traditions and created lavish Highland spectacles while evictions continued in Glen Garry, including that of the families of his Fencible Regiment on its disbandment in 1802. His behaviour as Highland Society President attracted the satire of Robert Burns in his 'Address of Beelzebub':

> But hear, my lord! Glengarry hear!
> Your hand's owre light on them, I fear;
> Your factors, grieves, trustees and bailies,
> I canna say but they do gaylies;
> They lay aside a' tender mercies,
> An' tirl the hullions to the birses;
> Yet while they're only poind and herriet,
> They'll keep their stubborn Highland spirit:
> But smash them! Crash them a' tae spails,
> An' rot the dyvors I' the jails...

Sir Walter Scott thought MacDonnell a 'treasure' and cast him as Fergus McIvor in his novel *Waverley* but to his people he was a disaster. MacDonnell opposed all modern projects, leading him to harry the builders of the Caledonian Canal that passed Invergarry House. On the west coast he evicted the successful livestock rearing family of Archibald Dhu of Kinlochnevis in 1817. He even rowed with the sheepmen who gave him most income to service his debts. Ironically he died in an accident in 1828 missing his footing and stepping off a steamer into the hated canal. By 1840 his successor had sold off all his patrimony to Lord Ward, apart from Knoydart.

Fifteen miles south-west on the A82 from Invergarry stands the Commando Memorial (NN 207824) to the soldiers of the 20th century who trained hereabouts for special duties in the Second World War. Take the B8004 three and a half miles west to Gairlochy and then the B8005 a similar distance north towards Achnacarry House, (NN 176878) the seat of Cameron of Locheil. The Gentle Locheil's vast Lochaber estates which had been forfeited for his part in the last Jacobite rising in 1745–46 were restored to his grandson in 1784. By the time of the latter's death in 1832, Glendessary, Glen Pean and Loch Arkaigside had been emptied of his clanspeople in favour of sheep. Many of the evicted people were 'driven to wretched hovels on the moss at Corpach' while able-bodied, young men enlisted in the British Army or emigrated. One thousand of them agreed to join Cameron of Erracht's Regiment in 1793 and fought throughout the French Wars. Others went less willingly in 1799, when the young Lochiel raised a Fencible Regiment by the customary method of threatening to evict their parents.

Many Lochaber Clearances were later blamed on estate factors but the truth is that, from Loch Arkaig to Loch Leven, the land was emptied of the Cameron clansfolk by their own chief, Locheil, to maintain his estate which at 76,000 acres remains the third largest in Inverness-shire. Some Cameron tacksmen made bids for their own land and became successful sheepmen. Another poorer Cameron surpassed them all. John Cameron of Coirechoille (NN 251806), near Roy Bridge, son of an innkeeper, became the greatest flock master in the north in the second and third decades of the 19th century. He rented sheep farms and prospered on lands once tenanted by his fellow clansmen. Some fragments of information about emigrant voyages from Lochaber can be found in the West Highland Museum, Cameron Square, Fort William (Tel: 01397 702169), but with few details about Clearance sites.

The deep fiords of Loch Linnhe, Loch Aline and Loch Sunart cut into the peninsula of Morvern, which lies around 25 miles south-west of Fort William. Drive nine miles south of Fort William on the A82, cross Loch Linnhe by the Corran Ferry and follow the A861 for 13 miles, to the junction of the A884 signposted for Lochaline. The former lands of the MacLean and MacDonald chiefs were severely ravaged after Culloden but the Campbell Dukes of Argyll sold on Morvern early in the 19th century. From the 1770s Morvern was a prime target for sheep walks but the lairds baulked at clearances till around 1815 but only tolerated the tenantry on narrow strips on the edge of the estate.

A few miles short of Lochaline take a minor road and drive three miles west to Kinloch. On the south side of Loch Doire nam Mart is a former township whose foundations are hidden in modern forestry. Aoineadh Mor (NM 660523) was cleared with many other townships in the 1820s. An old lady described it in detail to the Rev. Norman MacLeod, who recorded it in the Glasgow tenement where that evicted family had ended up and published it in English in the early 1860s: 'now only one smoke is to be seen, from the house of the Sassenach shepherd'.

The experienced hand of Patrick Sellar was applied to Morvern, where he hoped to become a laird in his own right. His first purchase with vacant possession was in 1838 at Acharn four miles north of Lochaline; he then added Clounlaid and Ulladail in 1841, and in 1844 he acquired the balance of the fishing rights on the River Aline and Ardtornish, along with a residence suitable for his family. At the time he controlled 32,000 acres and ran over 8,000 sheep. Of the 2,036 persons resident in Morvern parish at the time of the 1831 census, only 635 remained by 1911.

The B849 along the relatively sheltered mainland side of the Sound of Mull passes Savery and Keil, where 15 families were cleared between 1841 and 1851 by Mr J Sinclair's estate. From the Drimnin road end 12 miles on, a walk of two miles brings you to Auliston (NM

550571) where 105 souls from 21 families were cleared by Lady Gordon's factors in 1855.

You can retrace your steps north from Lochaline to Strontian and rejoin the A861 west towards Sunart and Ardnamurchan, or take the year-round ferry from Lochaline to Fishnish on the Isle of Mull, is the second largest island in the Inner Hebrides which is sometimes called 'The Officers' Mess'. Mull can also be reached by ferry from Oban. The population of Mull fell from 10,612 in 1812 to 6,441 in 1871. Parts of the island lost one-third to half of their people by eviction alone; many people, disillusioned and deprived of the opportunity to make a living, left for the cities.

Taking the A849 from Fishnish west it is 34 and a half miles to Bunessan on Loch na Lathaich on the coast of the Ross of Mull. Shiaba (NM 438192), a typical cleared township, is to be found three miles from Bunessan by a minor road to Scoor (NM 416193), then walk three quarters of a mile east. In 1838 some of the Shiaba tenants went to Ardalanish (NM 372193) along the coast and 12 families were moved on from there for another sheep farm, some to Ardtun, north of Bunessan. Many emigrated after the Duke of Argyll's rearrangements in the Ross of Mull (RC 34777-89) around 1848. Shiaba's 20 families in 1841 were reduced to four in 1861. We know that some of its former inhabitants did well in Canada. Friends back home were encouraged with letters to emigrate. Crops had been good and there was no factor to contend with. Others who fled during the famine died of disease on the journey.

The ancient remains of a chapel and a standing stone at nearby Scoor testify to the early and prolonged settlement of an area that was threatened with total clearance at the height of the potato famine in 1847. Some Shiaba tenants threatened with eviction petitioned the Duke who was assured by the factor that they would be given other crofts near Bunessan that had been vacated by earlier forced emigrants. This led to an act of resistance when they defied the factor and stayed put. However, bit by bit, one sheep farming tenant controlled more and more of the township. In the famine years of 1846 to 1852 over 600 summonses of removal and sequestration were issued for tenants on Mull estates.

Drive six and a half miles north from Fishnish to Salen on the A849 and turn west on the B8035 for two and a half miles and west, then take the B8073 along the north side of Loch na Keal. After six miles you see the small island of Ulva (NM 400400). It was stripped of 350 of its 500 people between 1847 to 1849 by the proprietor FW Clarke. Nine miles further on you can walk to Crackaig (NM 350464), an abandoned settlement whose walls stand almost complete in a fertile strath with spectacular views to Staffa and Iona and the Treshnish Isles that were cleared in 1802. You reach Crackaig by a two mile path starting from beside a ruined school-house on the B8073. The proximity to the school shows that the settlement was extant after the passage of the Education Scotland Act of 1872, when a school in every locality was built. Crackaig is two and a half miles south of Calgary Bay. Calgary, cleared in 1812, gave its name to the city in Alberta Canada, the destination of many Mull emigrants. Dervaig was emptied in 1857. Mishnish, near the port of Tobermory, was turned to sheep in 1842.

In summer there is an option to take the ferry from Tobermory to Kilchoan. Ardnamurchan, the most westerly part of the Scottish mainland, suffered substantial depopulation from the 1830s onwards. As in Morvern the lure of paid work in the industrialised south of Scotland tempted many to seek seasonal work in the cities and lowland farms. This is borne out by census records: for instance on 6 June 1841, 123 persons were temporarily absent on census day, and 35 people on 30 March 1851 were working away.

His mounting debt caused by his attempts to feed a destitute people, prompted the laird Sir James Riddell to apply for summons of removal in April 1852. 85 families in 12 townships were affected. Five miles north of Kilchoan some families were resettled on poor land at Sanna (NM 449692) on the tip of the peninsula. Riddell's estates ran 19 miles east along the B8007 to Salen on the north shore of Loch Sunart. Riddell had cleared small numbers throughout the previous 50 years to try to balance the books but he sold out in 1855 to John James Dalgleish. Many of his former tenants took emigrant ships that left Tobermory each year in the famine period.

Entering Inverness-shire beyond Acharacle on the A861, three miles north of Salen, the road takes you 19 miles along Loch Moidart and Loch Ailort, through a strongly Jacobite land that paid a heavy price for its loyalty to Bonnie Prince Charlie. As a penalty Moidart was passed from Clanranald to various landlords who cleared several sections. In 1851 many crofters emigrated to Canada from Loch Shiel estate. In the 1840s around the Sound of Arisaig, Lord Cranstoun cleared many townships, while Kinloid (NM 661880), a mile north of Arisaig, was cleared in 1853. The A830 winds six miles north to Mallaig, the port for Skye, the Small Isles and Lochboisdale, South Uist and Barra.

The MV *Western Isles* serves the scattered communities who live in the almost roadless peninsula around Loch Nevis. At Inverie (NM 766999) village, take the road to Airor on the Sound of Sleat. Knoydart, known as the Rough Bounds, is set between Loch Hourn and Loch Nevis facing Skye across the Sound of Sleat. Knoydart, Knut's fiord, from the Norse, experienced Clearances around 1750, carried out by the MacDonnells of Glengarry. In 1853 it was brutally cleared by the trustees of the impoverished and bankrupt MacDonnells. This Knoydart Clearance took place in the glare of publicity, with the harrowing details well documented. There was no succour from government for famine relief official referred to the 'parasitic population' of Knoydart. Having barely survived the potato famine of 1845–46, many people were in no fit state to pay rents, nor had they the capital to invest in fishing or other possible sources of income. Here, as at Arisaig and elsewhere, sheep farms, sometimes augmented by game and deer shooting, were deemed by the lairds and their trustees to be the most profitable form of land use.

Knoydart's permanent population dwindled under successive owners and by the 1890s only around 400 people lived there. Following the estate sale by the Bowlby family in 1934 it returned to prominence as the scene of the last land raid in Scotland in 1948. Seven ex-servicemen staked claims on the land of the pro-Nazi laird, Lord Brockett, but received no support from the post-war Secretary of State for Scotland for whom the 'continuation of crofting was incompatible with the type of agricultural progress' which the Labour government wished to encourage in the Highlands and

Islands. A succession of private owners failed to secure work for more than a few remaining inhabitants. The area remains a classic example of the man-made Highlands wildernesses created in the last 200 years. The Knoydart Land Raid Commemoration Committee raised a cairn at Inverie, one hundred yards from the pier in September 1991, at a ceremony which attracted around one-hundred people. The last of a string of unsuitable, private owners were forced to sell up and Knoydart was 'liberated from feudalism' on 26 March 1999 when 17,000 acres was bought by a consortium backing the community-based Knoydart Foundation. A new chapter has opened for the residents of this fragile, beautiful land, sometimes called 'the Highlands of the Highlands'.

# CHAPTER 7

# The Small Isles

REGULAR FERRIES SAIL from Mallaig and Arisaig to the Small Isles of Rum, Canna, Eigg and Muck. Rum is a nature reserve controlled by Scottish Natural Heritage for the study of deer. Permission is required from the warden to land at the pier in Loch Scresort (NM 408992) and for an overnight stay on the island. Rum was cleared in 1826 of its 400 people by MacLean of Coll; they emigrated to Cape Breton, provided with seven weeks subsistence for the harrowing voyage. The whim of subsequent wealthy owners was to keep Rum as a rich man's playground.

For much of the 20th century, the owner of Canna was John Lorne Campbell, who bequeathed the island to the National Trust for Scotland in perpetuity. Campbell wished to see the sea and land resources of the Hebrides in local hands. In the 1930s he had advocated a Sea League, following the Land League tradition. Writing in 1984 he condemned the Clearances:

> . . . (there was a) complete lack of security of tenure and compensation for improvements for small tenants before the Crofters' Act of 1886. Under such conditions there were immense opportunities for petty tyranny on the part of the factors and ground officers of absentee landlords in the highlands, who in those days had the entire force of the law behind them. To a Norwegian or an Icelander, accustomed to a free peasant society, the agrarian conditions that existed in the Highlands and Islands in the 18th and 19th centuries are quite incredible . . .

Before 1851 Canna experienced partial evictions, some voluntary, including 17 summonses in that year. The privations of the potato blight and sub-division of crofts consequent on a rising population on very limited land were the reasons behind the proprietor's writs.

The past oppression of the people of Eigg is a litany of factors' and landlords' whims. The pre-Culloden days were far from idyllic. Chiefs had the power of 'pit and gallows' over their clan. Clanranald's baillie Angus MacDonald of Laig (NM 467878) cleared small tenants off the neighbouring tack of Cleadale (NM 475890) for his tacksman brother-in-law from Knoydart who had hit hard times; consequently the former tenants-at-will left the island cursing the baillie. Eigg experienced all the ups and downs of kelping, fishing, crop failure, over-crowding, voluntary and enforced clearance and a string of absentee owners after Clanranald sold out in 1827. But in late 20th century history Eigg came under community control through the Isle of Eigg Heritage Trust. Today the residents are building a lively and sustainable life for the island, rooted in the Gaelic tradition with 21st century aspirations.

The crofters on the Isle of Muck, the smallest of the Small Isles, suffered a similar fate to those who lived on Rum. MacLean of Coll offered 150 people assistance to emigrate, but many of the former kelpers set up huts in the township of Keil by the harbour. They only managed to stave off emigration temporarily. There is lively community on the island today, but in numbers it is a far cry from the peasant native population of the clan era.

Burning cottage

# CHAPTER 8

# North and South Uist, Benbecula and Barra

THERE IS A FERRY to Lochboisdale on South Uist from Oban on several days each week. From there it is 43 miles by road (A865 and A867) to the North Uist port of Lochmaddy where there is a ferry terminal for Uig on Skye and Tarbert on Harris. Ten miles west of Lochmaddy, on the A865, lies Solas (NF 800740), the remains of a scattered crofting settlement that had 700 of its inhabitants evicted by the trustees of Lord MacDonald's estates in 1849. (A graphic contemporary description of this Clearance appeared in the *Inverness Courier* and was reproduced in Alexander MacKenzie's *Highland Clearances*.) The trustees were determined to increase estate incomes, Clanranald's inherited debt left him powerless, and only a few were able to crowd into poor land at Locheport to cling to their native land. The Solas evictions were notable for the resistance offered to the evictors, for the involvement of troops to protect the ground officers' desperate business of pulling down houses and for the public debate about the circumstances thereafter. Nevertheless many hundreds of North Uist people, in dire straits following the crisis of the potato blight, took assisted passage on dangerous and fever-ridden ships to Canada and Australia in 1850 and 1852.

At Lochmaddy itself (NF 920682) an eviction took place in 1895 from a dwelling near the Old Court House that was preserved on photographic plates. It is a graphic reminder of the rigours of such events. Eight miles west of Solas a successful land raid took place in 1952 at Balelone Farm (NF 728738). This resulted in the extension of some local holdings from the land of a Norfolk-based, absentee landowner, Lt. Col. Cator.

The A865 spinal route of the Southern Isles travel across the causeways built to link the islands during the World Wars. Millionaire

Aberdeen landlord Col. Gordon of Cluny bought Benbecula, South Uist and Barra from the bankrupt Clanranald in 1841. Driving past the sandy machair lands on the west coast and townships road ends such as those for Kildonan (NF 744278), Milton (NF 744263) and Frobost (NF 746252), pinpoints some cleared areas made-over into large farms. To the east over the rough high hills of South Uist that reach 620 m Beinn Mhor lie hidden glens like Corrodale (NF 833313). It is famed as a cave hideout of Bonnie Prince Charlie, before his return to Skye with Flora MacDonald of Milton, where the Church of Scotland minister took over a tack in the 1850s including Corrodale. The evicted tenant formerly kept 600 sheep and 30 cattle there, according his grandson Donald MacLennan, of Garrynamonie township, who gave evidence to Napier. Desperate to find a place to stay some of the men took boats 12 miles down the coast to Bay Harstavagh (NF 828155) and made turf cottages and broke in the heathery land. Six years later 13 families who had gathered there were moved again to the previously uncultivated, south side of the island of Eriskay (RC paras.11675-11698).

The South Uist crofting and cottar population doubled between 1755 and 1841 as the kelp industry was used to crowd people into coastal strips and sheep farming was expanded by the removal of hill grazings from crofting use. Gordon evicted 1,500 people from Benbecula, South Uist and Barra in 1851, after the famine, and forced them, some bound hand and foot, to board emigrant ships and remove them from his property. Another Napier Commission witness, John MacKay of Kilphedir described seeing a policeman chasing a young man. The lad hid on a little island but the police got a dog to flush him out. He was caught and sent off 'like an animal that was going to the southern markets' (RC paras 11088-11173). The hard-bitten Famine Relief Officers reported on Gordon's total lack of co-operation to combat starvation amongst his tenants. Contemporary Canadian newspapers remarked on the poverty of these emigrants even in comparison with paupers from the Irish poorhouses.

The islands of Barra and Vatersay, where few families had ever been moved from their homes, were first rented from the estate of

MacNeil of Barra and then bought by Gordon of Cluny. The population fell by a third in 50 years, the rest forced to make way for incoming tenants such as Dr McGillivray in 1850, who farmed a third of the island from Eoligary (NF 700071). He was accused of tyrannical practices towards the overcrowded crofters and cottars who had to squeeze into poor, worn-out patched of land that remained. It was said that near-starving people were even forbidden to collect cockles on the seashore. Many of them failed to grow enough to feed their families; having so little ground it was impossible to keep even a milk cow. They were forced into day labour on Dr MacGillivray's farm in return for bent grass to thatch their cottages. Some men tried to pay the rent as fishermen or in bad years as fish-curers for the big east coast fishing firms that working from the island.

Desperation led to land raiding; as a result Vatersay was bought by the government in 1910 and repopulated with descendants of people who had been cleared from the island under the Gordon/Cathcart regime. Vatersay has been joined by causeway to Barra in recent years to bring it into the bigger Barra community.

# CHAPTER 9

# Argyll, including Lorne, Islay, Jura, Colonsay, Gigha and Kintyre

CROSSING THE MINCH to Oban from Castlebay; Barra, Tiree and Coll are seen to the south before the ferry takes the sheltered route through the Sound of Mull towards the railhead port. The island of Tiree is owned by the Campbell Dukes of Argyll, whose estates extend to 60,800 acres. The Earls and then Dukes of Argyll owned much of Argyll, the homeland of the first Scottish Gaels. They became major players in Scottish and British politics down to the 20th century. In this county widespread 'Improvements', enclosures and amalgamations of holdings were in progress well before Culloden. As the first part of the Gaidhealtachd to come under southern influences and to become accessible to the steamers and trains of the Victorian transport revolution, depopulation was very severe. Between 1831 and 1911 Argyll lost half its population, a total of 30,000 people. Those who were crowded into the coastal villages took avidly to the radical politics of the *Oban Times* and elected a Land League MP in 1885.

In Tiree, 93 tenants and their families were cleared by the Duke of Argyll between 1846 and 1852 to reduce famine and reallocate land; at the same time as the Clearances which were happening on the Ross of Mull. However, after land raids and agitation which resulted in Marines being landed at the turn of the century, the Crofters' Commission and Congested District Board ordered a number of large amalgamated farms to be restored to crofting tenure. It is as a result of this policy that significant populations inhabit Tiree and other islands to this day.

The story on neighbouring Coll is far less happy. The land is less fertile and the laird MacLean of Coll was far less wealthy than his neighbouring proprietor, Argyll. So in the midst of the famine period, between 1846 and 1853, 92 families were evicted from Coll. Many others went voluntarily; as MacLean's factor informed the Court in Stornoway, these Coll people were desperate to break out of their rapidly deteriorating economic situation:

> ... from the failure of the potatoes and the low price of black cat-
> tle, they will be unable to preserve their stock entire and pay their
> rent; and, finding themselves falling back in the world, they desire
> to emigrate before their capital is too much reduced... (Richards,
> *Highland Clearances,* p.200)

Driving inland 26 miles on the A85, turn at the junction of the B8074 for Glenorchy where you see Ben Dorain 1076 m (NN 325379) which dominates the glen. This part of Argyll, the property of the Marquis of Breadalbane until the mid-19th century, suffered Clearances from around 1806 to 1831 along with his other estates. Glenorchy was the home of the famous Gaelic nature poet, Duncan Ban MacIntyre (1724–1808). His memorial in Greyfriar's Kirkyard commemorates his later life in Edinburgh, waking as a member of the town guard. His poem bemoaned the changes:

> I was in the mountain yesterday and my mind was full of the
> thoughts that the beloved ones, who were wont to be traversing
> the wilderness with me, were not there. And the Ben – it's little I
> thought that she would change! Since she is now under sheep, the
> world has deceived me! (translation)

Clearances took half of Glenorchy's people in the ten years from 1831, to make way for huge sheep farms. Despite this blow to morale, Free Church surveyors reported on the community solidarity they saw there in November 1846: tenants shared 'their own little stores most liberally with the destitute'. Few inhabitants remain today in this thinly-spread sheep-farming and sporting community.

From Dalmally at the mouth of Glenorchy, drive 15 miles south on the A85 via the A819, past Loch Awe, to reach Inveraray. This is a planned village built at a discreet distance from Inveraray Castle, seat of the Dukes of Argyll. Nearby Glen Shira was cleared of the small Campbell tenants for sheep, the main record being the parish minister's notes in the NSA.

Lochgilphead lies 25 miles south on the A83, on the edge of Knapdale where in the late 18th century the estate of Malcolm of Poltalloch benefitted from the investment of his Jamaican plantation profits. But in 1848 the then Poltalloch laird, Neil Malcolm, oblivious to public opinion, tried to force the emigration of some of his small tenants from Arichonan (NR 774908) that lies at the head of Caol Scotnish on Loch Sween. Their proposed destination was an assisted passage to a very inhospitable part of Australia. The tenants were able to resist the proposed destination, but not the Clearance. The action took place just south of the Crinan Canal on the route of the modern B8025. A crowd of around 60 men and women drove off the factors and sheriff's officers trying to deliver writs of removal. Amongst the leaders subsequently arrested and tried were two women who received eight-month jail sentences. Despite calls for military intervention, cooler heads among the authorities asked the Gaelic-speaking fiscal to reason with the people. The ruins of the Poltalloch mansion (NR 816965) are to be found half a mile west of the B8025 from the Crinan Canal going north to Kilmartin.

Islay is the largest and most fertile of the Southern Inner Hebrides. A ferry goes there from Kennacraig on West Loch Tarbert, which lies 19 miles south of Lochgilphead on the A83. Islay, Jura, Colonsay and Gigha all experienced the consolidation of farms and squeezing out of small tenants. Islay was the medieval capital of the MacDonald Lords of the Isles who ruled most of the Hebrides from their Loch Finlaggan capital. By the 19th century the Campbells of Islay, like many other native lairds, were seeking to improve their rental income through the introduction of sheep farming and the clearance of existing tenants.

The farm of Kilchiaran (NR 207603) was cleared in the 1820s of its nine tenants and their families and far more cottars. John Murdoch, future editor/owner of *The Highlander*, wrote with first-hand knowledge of the place, for he was brought up there:

... by false and foolish counsel the proprietor was induced to break up this prosperous little community. A Fifeshire farmer, supposed to be wealthy, came to the country to look for a farm. Kilchiaran was the one he coveted. The landlord, desirous of introducing the light of Lowland farming among his people, agreed to let the stranger have the land – even before the expiration of the leases by which the natives held it. He offered these natives farms elsewhere – an offer which some accepted. But whether they accepted or not, they were all turned out and dispersed and the Fifeshire man installed – not exactly in their place but in a new house and steading which were prepared for him.

Some of the old tenants went to law with the landlord and were ruined. Some went to America. One man, whom we met on our tour, is a miserable pauper in the country. And one, in his extremity, stole a few turnips from a field belonging to the proprietor, was imprisoned for the felony and died of disgrace and a broken heart. As a natural consequence, the humble cottiers were scattered to the four winds of heaven. And not one stone remains upon another to tell where their cosy hearths once blazed – excepting what we saw in one old sooty house. (J Murdoch, 1859 MS in the National Library of Scotland)

Clearances in the 1830s saw the emigration of 130 Islay people. In the decade from 1841, ten times as many were banished by the Campbell trustees. Particular areas affected at this time were the Glen and the Oa peninsula. Generally sheep farming came much later to Islay than to many other areas, but big farms and high rents did their inevitable business. The period beyond the famine years saw more consolidation and evictions under the Ramsay estate and others.

The ferry from Port Askaig sails across the narrow Sound of Islay to Feolin Ferry, Jura. The narrow A846 road covers only 16 miles on the east coast of the island. On the roadless west coast, the township of Cnocbreac (NR 449731) was cleared in the famine times. Each decade in the 19th century saw a population decrease on Jura; about a third of the Jura people were removed between 1841 and 1851.

The north part of Gigha (reached by ferry from Tayinloan on Kintyre) was gathered into a sheep farm, but many other Gigha folk continued to make a living from cod fishing or went to work at sea in the merchant navy.

The Isle of Colonsay is reached by ferry from Kennacraig via Islay, or from Oban. Sir John MacNeill, the third son of the Colonsay laird, played a major part in famine relief as first chairman of the Board of Supervision of the Scottish Poor Law, from 1845 to 1868. But his beliefs that the crisis of the famine should be used to teach 'indolent' Highlanders the moral and material benefits of self-dependence and industry were in the classic laissez-faire economics of his day. Sentiment be damned, succeed or emigrate, was the establishment's rationale!

It is 32 miles southwards on the A83 from Kennacraig to Campbeltown near the Mull of Kintyre. The uplands of the long peninsula were largely 'converted into an immense sheepwalk' in the late 18th century, with mixed farming, Lowland style, on the better ground. Details of Clearances and evictions in this area are scarce.

# CHAPTER 10

# Arran

ACROSS THE KILBRANDON SOUND east of Kintyre lies the Isle of Arran. From Kennacraig on West Loch Tarbert it is six miles on the B8001 to Claonaig ferry for Lochranza. Alternatively, journey from Glasgow 30 miles by road or by train to Ardrossan, Ayrshire, and take the ferry to Brodick on Arran's east coast.

North Glen Sannox (NS 005467) is reached by driving nine miles north of Brodick on the A841, or seven miles south of Lochranza. Here in 1829 and 1830 the Duke of Hamilton's estates evicted 29 families to make way for farming amalgamations designed to 'improve' the estate. Today the consequences can still be seen. Bracken infested hillsides and *fuar larachan* (cold hearths), or old house-sites, strung out along the north side of the glen. Laggantuin (NR 998486) is a clearly defined deserted village associated with the Glen Sannox Clearance. A minor road off the A841 (NG 008464) leads a picnic area at the mouth of the North Sannox Burn. Follow the shore track and path north and climb easy slopes to reach Laggantuin half a mile beyond the Fallen Rocks (NG 003483) on the shore track. Another interesting site is Cock Farm (NR 965513), reached by a two mile hill path from Lochranza. Here the Macmillan family lived for generations. However they were finally cleared from the island in 1814 after losing their share of a runrig farm at Achag, above Corrie. (Daniel Macmillan was born in 1813 and went on to found the famous book publishers MacMillan & Co. His great grandson was British Prime Minister from 1957–63.)

At Catacol, two miles south-west from Lochranza on the coast road there is a terrace of 12 cottages (NR 911497). Dubbed the 'twelve apostles', they were built to house the people cleared from Glen Catacol which was being turned over to deer shooting.

In the 1980s a researcher in Canada displayed photographs of North Glen Sannox, as it is today, to descendants of the dozens of

Arran families cleared from the island. These Scots-Canadians in Megantic County, Quebec, apparently could not believe that they had come from such poor ruins; surely their homes had been big houses and castles? This loss of contact with the reality of the Clearances is being replaced by more accurate knowledge, as descendants of the diaspora search for their ancestors.

Arran Heritage Museum, Rosa Burn, Brodick (NS 008367) contains relics of considerable interest. The pre-Clearance display shows where the old communal runrig farms were. There is a display of photographs of gravestones of people who emigrated from Arran to Megantic County, Canada. The museum is open daily in summer.

In the village of Lamlash a cairn has been erected to mark the spot (NS 028313) on the green in front of the estate cottages where an open air church service was held in 1830 for the emigrants of that year who embarked on the brig *Caledonia* for Quebec.

A minor road leaves the A841 south of Lamlash. It follows Monamore Glen in a south-westerly direction over the Ross into Glenscorrodale and along valley of the Sliddery Water over ten miles. This fertile strath was cleared as part of the Arran Estate reorganisations with many folk choosing to leave on assisted passage funded by the Duke of Hamilton for Chaleur Bay, Nova Scotia in the early 1830s. Gargadale (NR 957262) supported six families and was cleared in 1828. Glenscorrodale (NR 964280) had three tenants and Burican (NR 945292) had eight. While some families were found homes on the island, most left for the colonies.

A few miles further east along the A841 on a minor road to the west of Kilmory Water lie small farms at High Cloined (NR 965224), Aucheleffan (NR 980245) and on the east side take an off-road cycle route from the junction at (NR 970215) to reach Auchareoch (NR 994245). They were part of Celtic communal farms. Improvements thinned out tenants until the last were removed by forestry development in the 1960s.

# CHAPTER 11

# Perthshire

TRAVELLING FROM ARGYLL into Perthshire from the hills and lochs of the Blackmount via the A82 to Tyndrum you reach a large county of great contrasts. Many of the people of the upland areas of Perthshire once made a living by cattle rearing and selling, whisky-making and performing services to their clans. The Breadalbane branch of Clan Campbell dominated much of western Perthshire until the middle of the 19th century before mounting debt forced sales of much of their lands. Follow the A82 through Crianlarich. Eleven miles after joining the A85, you branch onto the A827 along the north side of Loch Tay. It is 17 miles on to Kenmore and Taymouth Castle (NN 784466) the former pile of the profligate Breadalbanes who entertained Queen Victoria to the delights of lavish, Highland sporting holidays. A further six miles on the A827 reaches the largest west Perthshire town, Aberfeldy, where the road branches south ten miles on the A826 and A822 to reach the old droving inn at Amulree (NN 900367). Loch Tayside and Glen Quaich were cleared before the middle of the 19th century; Glen Quaich lost 55 of its former 60 families. Keeping up with their cousins in Inveraray, the Breadalbane Campbells decided to raise their income from rents turning the estate over to sheep farming. Some efforts were made to resettle on the estate, but the 4th Marquis of Breadalbane still gained for himself a reputation like that of the 1st Duke of Sutherland.

The B846 north from Aberfeldy reaches Tummel Bridge near Loch Rannoch in 13 and a half miles. It can also be reached from the A9 (T) near Pitlochry, on the B8019 and B846, 30 miles west of Aberfeldy. It was first cleared by the trustees of the Forfeited Estates in the 1750s before being returned to the Robertsons of Struan. The Forfeited Estates administration protected to some extent the Black Wood of Rannoch with its ancient native pines, from the ravages of over-grazing by sheep and deer. There was increased demand for wood for building and fencing Perthshire's 'improved' farms. The Clan Donnachaidh Museum (NN 821661) sited at Bruar just off the A9 can provide some details about these lands that were cleared for sheep and deer forests.

In the domain of the Dukes of Atholl great changes were instigated from around 1750 onwards. In Glen Tilt tracks run 30 miles north from Bridge of Tilt (NN 876656) in Blair Atholl to where the Geldie Burn meets the Dee (NO 007867). Around 1784 the glen was virtually emptied to create a pleasure park for the Duke of Atholl.

The removals affected more occupations than crofting alone. For example, in the time of the Clearances, the Stewart lands at Glen Fincastle (NN 869623), when a shoemaker, millwright, or tailor died, retired or left, he was never replaced. Again and again, a reduction of skilled resident workers added to depopulation of the Highlands in the 19th century:

> A gradual run down in self-supporting communities in which local craftsmen were unable to compete economically with the mass-produced goods on sale in the nearest town, or hold their own either in resources or in skills with the larger firms.

Eight miles north-east from Pitlochry on the A924 lies Straloch in upper Strathardle, an area that was cleared by a cadet branch of clan Donnachie in 1824, with some degree of force, to make way for sheep.

# CHAPTER 12

# Strathspey and Badenoch

ALTHOUGH THE LOVAT FRASERS and the Seafields were more humane than many Clearance landlords, vast areas of this part of Scotland are now man-made wildernesses virtually empty of people. Deer forests have existed in the heart of the Grampian Mountains from early times.

Driving north on the A9 (T), or taking the train from Pitlochry, you pass Dalnaspidal at the mouth of Loch Garry (NN 646729). The steep slopes on the loch's south side show evidence of deforestation and over-grazing by the sight of prominent erosion gullies. In a mere ten years from around 1795, the introduction of sheep farming and the clearance of small tenants was effected, resulting in devastating changes to the landscape.

Travelling on through Drumochter Pass, take the A889. From Dalwhinnie to Laggan is the nine miles of Strath Mashie where sheep were introduced in the 1790s. Eight miles further north on the A86 is the village of Newtonmore. From a junction in the middle of the village (NN 713990) a minor road reaches Glen Banchor (pronounced Banachur) after two miles. This glen was cleared of seven families to make way for sheep. The Clan MacPherson Museum (Tel: 01540 673332), can be found in Newtonmore itself and Turus Tim on the northern outskirts is a part of the Highland Folk Museum in neighbouring Kingussie. These museums offer excellent material on past living conditions in the area. The Highland Folk Museum contains a reconstructed black house in addition to various model buildings; it is open all year.

The displacement of small numbers of families took place in many parts of Speyside from the late 18th century onwards. Glen Feshie was let as a deer forest in 1812 and Gaick, an age-old deer hunting ground reached along Glen Tromie that was itself converted from sheep to deer in 1826. Glen Tromie is the northern entry for two ancient drove routes to Atholl, Comyn's Road parallel with Drumochter, and further east through the Minigaig Pass to Glen Bruar. Many such routes became contentious during the shooting season in autumn at the very time cattle were driven to Lowland trysts, such as Falkirk, over these age-old, toll-free paths.

Glen Avon (pronounced A'an), whose waters rise on the north slopes of Cairngorm, was cleared successively for deer in 1838 and 1841 is best reached from the A939 at Tomintoul or over the Lecht at Corgarff.

Glenmore, situated seven miles east of Aviemore, is the all-year round, outdoor sports resort of Badenoch and Strathspey. At the foot of the Cairngorm mountains, and containing Loch Morlich and the ancient Rothiemurchus pine woods, Glenmore was cleared of its people in 1827 by the Duke of Gordon to make way for grouse shooting and then in 1843 for deer forest. This aristocratic pleasure seeker built the original Glenmore Lodge (NH 986094). The Glenmore people were settled at The Street, Boat of Garten (NH 943189), seven miles away. The Gordon family sold the estate to the Forestry Commission in 1923.

A Western Isles blackhouse

# CHAPTER 13

# Deeside and Angus Glens

IN THE UPPER GLENS of the eastern Highlands there were removals of people from the early 18th century by various Deeside lairds, again lured by the profits that could be made from leasing the land for deer shooting and sheep farms. But in this area places for the cleared tenants were often found on other parts of the estates.

From the north-west, approach Deeside via Donside via the Lecht from Strathspey. From Blairgowrie in the south, take the A93 road 35 miles to Braemar. It follows the Ericht/Black Water/Allt a' Glinne Bhig, a south flowing tributary of the Tay, up Glenshee to the Devil's Elbow where a formerly tight hairpin bend on the road has been removed. From the watershed at 665 m the route of the old military road leads north down Glen Clunie to Braemar.

In 1733 an attempted Clearance at Baddoch (NO 132828) was thwarted by legal challenge to ownership of the land, but Glen Clunie was subsequently cleared of 12 families who herded 2,000 sheep and 500 cattle to make way for two large sheep farms. The main A93 bridges a side stream, the Callater burn, (NO 157882) at the mouth of Glen Callater that had been uninhabited except for summer sheilings. It became a game preserve in 1884.

A minor road five miles west of Braemar leads to the Lynn of Dee (NO 061897). From here, gated roads lead west into Glen Dee and north into Glen Lui. The latter glen was cleared of four farms in 1726 by Lord Grange, the Hanoverian brother of John Erskine, forfeited as Earl of Mar for leading the 1715 Rising. A further Clearance took place in 1776 giving over Luibeg exclusively for deer. C Cordiner wrote in *Antiquities and Scenery of the North of Scotland* (1780), 'The ruins of several stone buildings shew that it had once been inhabited; but it is now, as the other pastures in the forest, left to fatten the deer.'

In the 1790s Glen Dee was more important for deer stalking than Glen Ey. *The Records of Invercauld*, 1901, by JC Michie, records that seven townships in Glen Dee 'carried a great stock of cattle and sheep, and in the remotest parts of the Mar forest, the people had their summer pasturages and sheilings, full of healthy human activity.' Yet the House of Commons Select Committee on Game Laws and Deer Forests in 1872 was told by the factor that the people had to been removed to low ground because of recurrent outbreaks of typhus and diphtheria: '. . . because the only food that they had was unripened cereals and unripened potatoes.' Clearly major changes in diet and economic circumstances had occurred, partly due to the slump in stock prices following the victory against Napoleon in 1815. The removal of upland summer grazings must have led to a drastic cut in the people's cattle and sheep stock, so reducing their circumstances and undermining their health. Also harsh winters occurred in 1782–3, 1795–6, 1806–7, 1816–17, and 1836–7 and emergency supplies of meal were imported, to relieve several parts of the West Highlands. The increasing dependence on the potato crop for subsistence made the potato blight of 1846–50 a widespread disaster. The demand for game shooting among the aristocracy sealed the fate of the indigenous people of the upland glens and straths.

Driving a mile and a half back from the Linn of Dee towards Braemar you pass by Inverey (NO 083893) at the mouth of the glen. Nine families were removed from Glen Ey around 1830. The plots of land near the village of Braemar, contrary to the reports given by estate spokesmen to the Select Committee, were far inferior to their previous land.

On the A93 on the north side of the river, about seven miles east of Braemar, the Gelder Burn (NO 242942) joins the River Dee. Glen Gelder was part of the Balmoral estate, leased to the Price Consort in 1848 and then sold to him in 1852 by the Earl of Fife's trustees. He then developed Balmoral Castle (NO 256952) as the model for all aspiring wealthy sportsmen, with its legions of estate workers, deer watchers and ghillies; gone was the free peasantry in the glens. A shooting tenant had already restricted summer grazings in 1830.

The removal of 13 families from the glen was organised under the Prince Consort's ownership of the estate. They were offered work on the estate that was developed exclusively as a sporting preserve.

Earlier in the 19th century Christian Watt – as was the age-old custom – used to walk miles far inland from her Fraserburgh home to sell dried fish. Much later she wrote of the Deeside Clearances. She and the other fisher-wives sold their wares to lairds and crofters alike and 'danced on the green at the castle of Mar in the moonlight'. The crofters in the upper reaches of the Dee spoke Gaelic and some Doric, the Aberdeenshire Scots tongue, but no English. These customers were cut off and removed by the advent of the sporting estate. Deer forests were set up and the hill roads were prohibited to travellers. Then the Earl of Fife and others landowners cleared the people. Christian Watt met two of her former customers years later on an Aberdeen street. Andrew Coutts and his friend Alex Ruanach were by then both granite masons. She recalled:

> I had known them when we were all bairns. They told me Lord Fife had cleared the whole glen to make a deer forest. All had to go on three months notice. Lord Fife's uncle was an honourable man who would have never evicted anybody, but now they were building vast palaces in relentless pursuit of pleasure, at the expense of a race who had probably been there since the end of the ice age. Both boys vowed vengeance, and said the day would come when the Skene Duffs (Fife's family name) would call on the mountains to fall upon them.

To reach the mouth of Glen Tannar, cross to the south side of the Dee at Crathie and take the B796 17 miles east towards Bridge o' Ess (NO 504972); a road goes to the heart of the glen in two miles south-west of this point. Two major evictions took place here in the 19th century. The craze for sport dictated that around 1850, 29 households were removed from the south side of the glen, while several other families were cleared between 1855 and 1858, removing some 7,000 of their sheep as a consequence. Many former tenants were found land in other parts of the then Huntly estates.

Continuing east on the B973, join the B974 and travel 25 miles

south across the Cairn o' Mount (369 m) to Fettercairn in the Howe
of the Mearns. Four miles south-west the B966 reaches the junction
near Ganochy (NO 600706) for Glen Esk in the county of Angus.
The road leads ten miles north-west into the heart of the glen to
Auchronie. The remains of large numbers of dwellings show the
scale of the population sustained in Glen Mark and Glen Lee,
upland offshoots of upper Glen Esk, before Clearances for sheep in
the late 18th century. The few sheep tenants and their 8,000 sheep
that grazed the slopes of the most easterly Munro, Mount Keen
939m, were removed in 1853 by the Earl of Dalhousie 'to make
room for deer' after their sheep farming leases terminated. An old
drove road from Ballater and Glen Tannar was also used for smug-
gling whisky in pre-Clearance times, as was Jock's Road further
west. It led from Braemar via Glen Callater and into Glen Clova
en route for Forfar and Dundee.

# CHAPTER 14

# Orkney

SIXTEEN OF THE Orkney Isles are inhabited today. The group, set ten miles from the Caithness coast, presented a contrast between a farming economy on one hand and an economy of crofter-fishermen on the other. However, they experienced in common the greed and arbitrary power of landlords from the days of Earl Patrick in the 17th century to the 'Little General' Burroughs in the 19th century. Exploitation here was as callous as anywhere else in the Highlands and Islands; and the details are coming to light through painstaking modern scholarship born of a renewed interest in the life of earlier generations of Orcadians whose distinctive Norse culture is being revived and fostered today.

The Orkney Islands (which are reached by ferry from Scrabster and Gills Bay in Caithness and from Aberdeen) also contain the sites of 19th century Clearances, particularly on the island of Hoy. In some respects, however, Orkney does not highlight the severity of the Clearances elsewhere in the Highlands and Islands as the old Norse 'udal' system of land tenure on the Orkneys afforded some protection from depopulation by eviction. A prime example of the tyrannical power of feudal landlordism was shown in the case of the eviction of Rousay crofter, James Leonard by General Burroughs after he had given evidence to the Napier Commission in 1886. WPL Thompson recounts the full story in *The Little General and the Rousay Crofters*. The largest single Clearance in Orkney also took place in Rousay, when (in 1845) General Burrough's uncle George William Traill, known in India as the 'King of Kumaon', cleared 200 people from Quandal, where the remains of their runrig farming system are still clearly visible. Quandal lies just beyond one of the finest concentrations of archeological remains in Scotland including well-preserved Neolithic chambered cairns from 3,500 BC. With the Clearance of Quandal, a single, arrogant Victorian laird brought 5,500 years of continuous human settlement to an abrupt end.

# CHAPTER 15

# Shetland

ROUTES ARE EXPENSIVE by air and cheaper, longer and choppier by ferry from Aberdeen. There are 14 inhabited islands in Shetland. The principal town, Lerwick, is situated on Mainland. The Library and Museum, Lower Hillhead, Lerwick provides information on the Clearances on the islands. Their publication, *Shetland from Old Photographs* in 1978, shows a remarkable pair of photographs of the township of Garth near Quendale. One shows the houses, stacks and in-bye land just prior to the eviction of 27 households in 1874 to make way for sheep and the second, taken in 1880, shows the same scene, now cleared for sheep and almost totally devoid of any trace of human life. The *Braer* tanker disaster in early 1993 occurred on the cliffs close to this site.

The small island of Fetlar, in the north-east of the Shetland group, is a microcosm of 19th century landlord tyranny. The Clearances of 1822 and 1870 by the Nicolsons of Brough emptied the whole of the west side of Fetlar. 'The principle used was to erect a stone wall closing off a particular part of the island. Then when the wall was complete, the people were given 40 days to remove themselves' (RL Johnston, *The Deserted Homesteads of Fetlar*, Shetland, Shetland Life, 1981). In 1822 the first of many walls cut off the Lamb Hoga peninsula (HU 600900). However, many of the laird's agricultural experiments were disastrous and a lease of the island between 1833 and 1840 forced people to sell their fish and cattle exclusively to the new tenants. Over a 31 year period more than 300 people were evicted and scattered. Unst and Yell had similar experiences of oppression and wall building to remove the people as detailed by Brian Smith in his book *Toons and Tenants*.

# Bibliography

THE LITERATURE OF the Clearances has grown remarkably in the past thirty years. The following books are recommended to explore in detail the people and places included in this guide.

## HISTORY & REFERENCE

Tom Atkinson, *The Empty Lands*, Edinburgh, Luath Press, 1986

Patrick Bailey, *Orkney*, Newton Abbot, Pevensey Press, 1995

Malcolm Bangor-Jones, *The Assynt Clearances*, Dundee, The Assynt Press, 1998

Thurso Berwick, (Morris Blythman) in *Rebel's Ceilidh Song Book*, Boness, 1976

Joni Buchanan, *The Lewis Land Struggle*, Stornoway, Acair, 1996

James Boswell, *Journal of A Tour to the Hebrides*

Andrew Boyle, *Pictorial History of Arran*, Darvel, Alloway Publishing, 1994

JM Bumstead, *The Peoples' Clearance: Highland Emigration to British North America 1770–1815*, Edinburgh, Edinburgh University Press, 1982

John Lorne Campbell, *Canna: The Story of a Hebridean Island*, Edinburgh, Canongate, 1994

AD Cameron, *Go Listen to the Crofters*, Stornoway, Acair, 1986

Derek Cooper, *Skye*, London, Routledge and Kegan Paul, 1970

David Craig, *On the Crofters Trail*, London, Jonathan Cape, 1990

David Craig and David Paterson, *The Glens of Silence – Landscapes of the Highland Clearances*, Birlinn, 2004

TM Devine, *Clanship to Crofters War – The Social Transformation of the Scottish Highlands*, Manchester, Manchester University Press, 1994

TM Devine, *The Great Highland Famine*, Edinburgh, John Donald, 1988

Diary of a Lewis Factor, extracts *West Highland Free Press* in the
issues throughout 1988

Camille Dressler, *Eigg: the Story of an Island*, Edinburgh,
Polygon, 1998

*As an Fhearann (From the Land): A century of images of the
Scottish Highlands*, Stornoway, Acair, 1986

W Forsyth, *In the Shadow of the Cairngorms*, Northern Counties
Publishing Co. 1900

Iain Fraser Grigor, *Mightier than a Lord*, Stornoway, Acair 1979

Phillip Gaskell, *Morvern Transformed*, Cambridge, Cambridge,
CUP, 1968

Rob Gibson, *Crofter Power in Easter Ross, 1884–1886*,
Dingwall, Highland Heritage, 1986

Rob Gibson, *The Promised Land*, Broadford, Strollamus Crofters
Defence Committee, 1974

Rob Gibson, *Toppling the Duke: Outrage on Ben Bhraggie*,
Evanton, Highland Heritage Books, 1996

James Shaw Grant, *A Shilling for your Smile*, Stornoway, Acair,
1992

Ian Grimble, *The Scottish Islands*, Edinburgh, BBC, 1985

Ian Grimble, *The Trial of Patrick Sellar*, London, RKP, 1962 &
Edinburgh, Saltire Society, 1992

Ian Grimble, *The Sutherland Story: Fact and Fiction*, in *Sar
Ghaidheal: Essays in honour of Ruaridh MacKay*, An
Comunn Gaidhealach, Inverness, 1986

Donald Gunn & Muriel Spankie, *The Highland Clearances*,
Eastbourne, Wayland Publishers in co-operation with BBC
Scotland Education, 1993

Harry Harrison, *Urchany and Farley, Leanassie and Breakachy:
parish of Kilmorack 1700–1998*, St Albans, printed for
private circulation, 1998

James Hunter, *The Making of the Crofting Community*,
Edinburgh, John Donald, 1976

James Hunter and Caillean MacLean, *Skye: The Island*,
Edinburgh, Mainstream 1986

James Hunter, *Scottish Highlanders: A People and Their Place*, Edinburgh, Mainstream Publishing, Edinburgh 1992

James Hunter, *A Dance Called America*, Edinburgh, Mainstream 1994

James Hunter, *'On the Other Side of Sorrow': Nature and People in the Scottish Highlands*, Edinburgh, Mainstream, 1995

James Hunter, *The Claim of Crofting*, Edinburgh, Mainstream, 1991

Robert L Johnston, *'The Deserted Homesteads of Fetlar'*, Shetland, Shetland Life, 1981

Jim Johnstone, *Tongue and Farr*, North Coast Enhancement Group/HIDB, 1984

Billy Kay, *Odyssey, Voices from Scotland's Recent Past*, Edinburgh, Polygon, 1980

Lerwick Library and Museum, *Shetland from Old Photographs*, 1978

John Lister-Kaye, *Ill Fares The Land*, Isle of Skye, Barail, 1990

Michael Lynch, *Scotland: A New History*, London, Century, 1991

Hugh MacDiarmid, ed., *Golden Treasury of Scottish Poetry* London Macmillan, 1948. It contains a translation of Duncan Ban MacIntyre, *Ode to Ben Dorain*.

Donald MacDonald, *Lewis: A History of the Island*, Edinburgh, Gordon Wright, 1978. A recent general history with references to Clearance areas.

Archie MacDougall, *Knoydart: The Last Scottish Land Raid* Cleveland, Lyndhurst, 1993.

John McEwen, *Who Owns Scotland*, Edinburgh, Polygon 1977

John MacGrath, *The Cheviot, the Stag and the Black, Black Oil*, Kyleakin, West Highland Publishing Co., 1974

Allan I Macinnes, *Clanship, Commerce and the House of Stuart, 1603–1788*, East Linton, Tuckwell, 1996

Alexander MacKenzie, *The Highland Clearances*, 1883 (Mercat Press reprint, 1997

Sorley MacLean, *'Hallaig & The Poetry of the Clearances'*, *Transactions of the Gaelic Society of Inverness* XXXVIII, 1939

Robert MacLellan, *The Isle of Arran*, Newton Abbot, David and Charles, 1968

Donald MacLeod, *Gloomy Memories*, reprinted Strathnaver Museum, 1982

Duncan Macmillan, 'Monumental struggle', *The Scotsman* 20 May 1996

IMM Macphail, *The Crofters' War*, Stornoway, Acair, 1989

Edward Meldrum, *From Nairn to Loch Ness*, Inverness, Inverness Field Club, 1980

John Murdoch, *For the People's Cause*, James Hunter, Edinburgh, HMSO, 1986

The Napier Commission, *Report of Royal Commission on Crofting* Edinburgh, HMSO, 1884

Helen Nicolson, *Clyth*, Clyth Community Association, 2004

James R Nicolson, *Shetland*, 4th Edition, Newton Abbot, David & Charles, 1984

Donald Omand, ed., *The Ross-shire Book*, Golspie, 1988

Willie Orr, *Deer Forests, Landlords and Crofters*, Edinburgh, John Donald, 1982

Willie Orr, *Discovering Argyll, Mull and Iona* Edinburgh, John Donald, 1990

John Prebble, *The Highland Clearances*, London, Secker & Warburg, 1963

John Prebble, *John Prebble's Scotland*, London, Secker and Warburg, 1984

Eric Richards, *Patrick Sellar and the Highland Clearances*, Edinburgh, Polygon Books, 1999

Eric Richards, *The Leviathan of Wealth*, London, Routledge and Kegan Paul, 1973

Eric Richards *The Highland Clearances* Edinburgh, Birlinn, 2000

Dr Ian Richardson, *One for the Pot* Laggan, Laggan Community, 1999

Denis Rixson, *Knoydart: A History*, Edinburgh, Birlinn, 1999

Rev. Donald Sage, *Memorabilia Domestica*, republished in paperback, 1981

Peter Seddon, 'Clearance Drawings', Edinburgh, *Cencrastus*, Autumn 1983

Brian Smith, *Toons and Tenants: Settlement and society in Shetland 1299 – 1899*, Shetland times 2000

Robert Somers, *Letters from the Highlands* (originally published in 1846) Inverness, Melven Press, 1980

Katharine Stewart, *Crofters and Crofting*, Glasgow, William Blackwood, 1980

William Taylor, *Glen Fincastle 1841–1901: A Study of a Perthshire Glen*, Edinburgh, Oliver & Boyd, 1967

WPL Thompson, *The Little General and the Rousay Crofters*, Edinburgh, John Donald, 1981

Francis Thompson, *Crofting Years*, Edinburgh, Luath Press, 1984

Francis Thompson, *The Victorian and Edwardian Highlands from Old Photographs*, London, Batsford, 1976

Francis Thompson, *Uists and Barra*, Newton Abbot, Pevensey Press, 1999

*The Times*, May 1845, Anonymous correspondent at Croick, copy on display in Croick Church.

'Ulva Clearance story', *Scots Magazine*, September 1984

Adam Watson and Elizabeth Allan, Depopulation by Clearances and Non-Enforced Emigration in the North East Highlands, Aberdeen, *Northern Studies* 10, 1990

Andy Wightman, *Who Owns Scotland*, Edinburgh, Canongate, 1996

Elly Williamson, *The Leckmelm Evictions*, Ullapool Museum, 2003

## NOVELS ASSOCIATED WITH THE HIGHLAND CLEARANCES

Kathleen Fiddler, *The Desperate Journey*, Edinburgh, Kelpie Books, 1984

Neil M Gunn, *Butchers Broom*, London, Souvenir Press, 1977

Mollie Hunter, *A Pistol in Greenyards*, London, Hamilton, 1988

Fionn MacColla, *And the Cock Crew*, New Edition, Edinburgh, Canongate, 1995

Allan Campbell McLean, *Ribbon of Fire*, Edinburgh, Kelpie, 1985

Allan Campbell McLean, *The Year of the Stranger*, London, Collins, 1971

Allan Campbell McLean, *A Sound of Trumpets*, London, Collins, 1971

Margaret McPherson, *The Battle of the Braes*, London, Collins, 1972

Iain Crichton Smith, *Consider the Lilies*, London, Gollancz, 1968

## VIDEO

*The Blood is Strong,* a joint Grampian TV/Channel 4 production that was first screened in September 1988. The three-part history charted the history of Gaelic Scotland to the present day. It contains excellent footage on the Clearances. A book, the music and a video of the series were produced.

# Some other books published by **LUATH** PRESS

## Plaids and Bandanas
Rob Gibson
ISBN 0 946487 88 X  PB  £7.99

What drew Highlanders to the cowboy life?

What did Scots do at the Battle of Little Bighorn?

How did Scots help to shape the culture of the West?

How did the music develop and who else influenced the development of the old songs?

From droving to driving, reivers to rustlers, heilan kye to long horns, *Plaids and Bandanas* explores the links between the two cattle cultures in music, song and dance, and folklore. The vast number of Scots who emigrated to North America has been well documented, whether through forcible eviction during the Clearances of the 18th and 19th centuries or voluntarily in the hope of a better life. With them they took their culture, their language, their music and their skills. Cattle droving in Scotland was an established profession from the 16th century, and many such migrants took cowboy jobs in the American West.

The medium of music paints a vivid picture of their social and personal lives and the exchange was not all one way. The music crossed and re-crossed the Atlantic creating strong links between the old culture and the new. Lonely men in strange surroundings found comfort in songs that reminded them of home.

Rob Gibson, himself a musician, knows the power of song. It has a unique ability to evoke and capture emotion and a sense of time and place. He has researched the roots of the songs and the routes of the drovers, and established clear and coherent links between the Wild West and the no-less-wild Highlands.

*Go beyond Hollywood cliché and learn the truth is even more colourful and fascinating. Plaid or bandana, the cattle trade was an international brotherhood and sisterhood whose story has now finally been explored: with humour and sensitivity.*
TOM BRYAN

*The result is an absorbing, thought provoking and informative book, rich in colour and humour and, like all good stories of adventure, a rollicking good read.*
ROSS-SHIRE JOURNAL

*He debunks the mythical version of the 'Wild West', replacing it with a history that is every bit as thrilling as Hollywood fictions.*
AM BRATACH

## The Highland Geology Trail

John L. Roberts

ISBN 0 946487 36 7  PB  £5.99

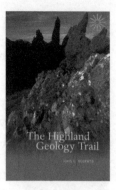

Where can you find the oldest rocks in Europe?

Where can you see ancient hills around 800 million years old?

How do you tell whether a valley was carved out by a glacier, not a river?

What are the Fucoid Beds?

Where do you find rocks folded like putty?

How did great masses of rock pile up like snow in front of a snow-plough?

When did volcanoes spew lava and ash to form Skye, Mull and Rum?

Where can you find fossils on Skye?

This journey of geological discovery through the diverse landforms of the north and west Highlands of Scotland offers the answers to these and many other questions of interest to visitors and local residents alike.

*Great care has been taken to explain specific tersm as they occur and, in so doing, John Roberts has created a resource of great value which is eminently usable by anyone with an interest in the outdoors... the best bargain you are likely to get as a geology book in the foreseeable future.*

PRESS AND JOURNAL

## The Story of Loch Ness

Katharine Stewart

ISBN 1 84282 083 4   HB   £16.99

Known throughout the world for its legendary
inhabitant, Loch Ness has inspired folklore and fas-
cination in the hearts of those who visit it for centuries. But what of the characters, the history and
the myths which enchanted inhabitants and travellers alike long before the first sightings of the so-
called Loch Ness Monster? Katharine Stewart takes
us on a journey through the past and the politics, the
heroes and the villains, and the natural beauties that
are the true source of the magic of Loch Ness.

Where did the name Loch Ness come from, and how did Cherry Island come to
be? What can be said of the wildlife that makes its home around the loch? Who
determined the fate of the Loch Ness valley as we know it today?

While the depths and secrets of Loch Ness may never be revealed entirely,
Stewart provides the answers to these and so many other questions in this com-
pelling guide to one of Scotland's most famous places.

*This delightful study of Loch Ness is written with deep knowledge and a lifetime of*
*love of one of the most wonderful spots in the Scottish Highlands.*
TC SMOUT

## Tunnel Tigers

Patrick Campbell

ISBN 1 84282 072 9 £8.99 PB

*Tunnel Tigers* is a colourful portrait of the off-beat characters who worked on Scottish hydro projects, and of the tensions that were created when men of various religious and ethnic groups shared the same space.

Tunnel tigers are an elite group of construction workers who specialise in a highly paid but dangerous profession: driving tunnels through mountains or underneath rivers or other large bodies of water, in locations as far apart as Sydney and San Francisco. At the turn of the last century they tunnelled out the subways under New York and London; in the 1940s and 1950s they were involved in a score of huge hydroelectric tunnels in Pitlochry and the Highlands of Scotland. They continue with their dangerous craft today in various locations all over the world.

Many of these daring men were born in north west Donegal, Ireland, where the tunnel tigers were viewed as local folk heroes because they had the bravado to work in dangerous conditions that few other working men could endure.

*I found the book of absorbing interest and read it straight through in one reading...*

ERIC McKEEVER

## The Hydro Boys

Emma Wood

ISBN 1 84282 047 8 PBK £8.99
ISBN 1 84282 016 8 HBK £16.99

'The hydro-electric project was a crusade, with a marvellous goal: the prize of affordable power for all from Scottish rainfall'

*'This book is a journey through time, and across and beneath the Highland landscape...it is not just a story of technology and politics but of people.'* EMMA WOOD

*'I heard about drowned farms and hamlets, the ruination of the salmon-fishing and how Inverness might be washed away if the dams failed inland. I was told about the huge veins of crystal they found when they were tunnelling deep under the mountains and when I wanted to know who 'they' were: what stories I got in reply! I heard about Poles, Czechs, poverty-stricken Irish, German spies, intrepid locals and the heavy drinking, fighting and gambling which went on in the NoSHEB contractors' camps.'*
EMMA WOOD

*Nobody should forget the human sacrifice made by those who built the dams all those years ago. The politicians, engineers and navvies of the era bequeathed to us the major source of renewable energy down to the present day. Their legacy will continue to serve us far into the 21st century.*

BRIAN WILSON MP, Energy Minister, announcing a 'new deal for hydro' which now 'provides 50 per cent of the UK's renewable energy output. The largest generator serves more than 4 million customers.'
THE SCOTSMAN

## Lewis and Harris: History and Pre-History

Francis Thompson

ISBN 0 946487 77 4  PB  £5.99

The fierce Norsemen, intrepid missionaries and mighty Scottish clans – all have left a visible mark on the landscape of Lewis and Harris. This guide explores sites of interest, from pre-history through to the present day.

Harsh conditions failed to deter invaders from besieging these islands or intrepid travellers from settling, and their legacy has stood the test of time in an array of captivating archaeological remains, from the stunningly preserved Carloway Broch to a number of haunting standing stones, tombs and cairns. Telling captivating tales of the places he visits – including an intriguing murder mystery and a romantic encounter resulting in dramatic repercussions for warring clans – Francis Thompson introduces us to his homeland and provides a fascinating insight into its forgotten way of life.

## Heartland

John MacKay

ISBN 1 905222 11 4 PBK £6.99

This was his land. He had sprung from it and would surely return to it. Its pure air refreshed him, the big skies inspired him and the pounding seas were the rhythm of his heart. It was his touchstone. Here he renourished his soul.

A man tries to build for his future by reconnecting with his past, leaving behind the ruins of the life he has lived. Iain Martin hopes that by returning to his Hebridean roots and embarking on a quest to reconstruct the ancient family home, he might find new purpose.

But as Iain begins working on the old blackhouse, he uncovers a secret from the past, which forces him to question everything he ever thought to be true.

Who can he turn to without betraying those to whom he is closest? His ailing mother, his childhood friend and his former love are both the building – and stumbling – blocks to his new life.

Where do you seek sanctuary when home has changed and will never be the same again?

*A fine, rewarding read.*
SUNDAY HERALD

## ISLANDS

**The Islands that Roofed the World: Easdale, Belnahua, Luing & Seil**
Mary Withall
ISBN 0 946487 76 6  PB  £4.99

**Rum: Nature's Island**
Magnus Magnusson
ISBN 0 946487 32 4  PB  £7.95

## LUATH GUIDES TO SCOTLAND

**The North West Highlands: Roads to the Isles**
Tom Atkinson
ISBN 1 84282 086 9  PB  £5.99

**Mull and Iona: Highways and Byways**
Peter Macnab
ISBN 0 946487 58 8  PB  £4.95

**The Northern Highlands: The Empty Lands**
Tom Atkinson
ISBN 1 84282 087 7  PB  £5.99

**The West Highlands: The Lonely Lands**
Tom Atkinson
ISBN 1 84282 088 5  PB  £5.99

## WALK WITH LUATH

**50 Classic Routes on Scottish Mountains**
Ralph Storer
ISBN 1 84282 091 5  PB  £6.99

**Skye 360: Walking the coastline of Skye**
Andrew Dempster
ISBN 0 946487 85 5  PB  £8.99

**The Joy of Hillwalking**
Ralph Storer
ISBN 1 84282 069 9  PB  £7.50

**Scotland's Mountains before the Mountaineers**
Ian R. Mitchell
ISBN 0 946487 39 1  PB  £9.99

**Mountain Days & Bothy Nights**
Dave Brown & Ian R. Mitchell
ISBN 0 946487 15 4  PB  £7.50

**Of Big Hills and Wee Men**
Peter Kemp
ISBN 1 84282 052 4  PB  £7.99

**Hill Walks in the Cairngorms**
Ernest Cross
ISBN 1 84282 092 3  PBK  £4.99

**Easy Walks in Monarch of the Glen Country: Badenoch and Strathspey**
Ernest Cross
ISBN 1 84282 093 1  PBK  £4.99

**Short Walks on Skye**
Joanna Young
ISBN 1 84282 065 6  PBK  £4.99

## HISTORY

**Scotch on the Rocks: The true story behind Whisky Galore**
Arthur Swinson
ISBN 1 905222 09 2  PB  £7.99

**Braveheart: From Hollywood to Holyrood**
Lin Anderson
ISBN 1 84282 066 4  PB  £7.99

**Reportage Scotland: Scottish history in the voices of those who were there**
Louise Yeoman
ISBN 1 84282 051 6  PB  £7.99

**Desire Lines: A Scottish Odyssey**
David R. Ross
ISBN 1 84282 033 8  PB  £9.99

**Scots in the USA**
Jenni Calder
ISBN 1 905222 06 8  PB  £8.99

**Scots in Canada**
Jenni Calder
ISBN 1 84282 038 9  PB  £7.99

## NATURAL WORLD

**Listen to the Trees**
Don MacCaskill
ISBN 0 946487 65 0   PB   £9.99

**Red Sky at Night**
John Barrington
ISBN 0 946487 60 X   PB   £8.99

**Wild Lives: Otters**
Bridget MacCaskill
ISBN 0 946487 67 7   PB   £9.99

**Wild Lives: Foxes**
Bridget MacCaskill
ISBN 0 946487 71 5   PB   £9.99

**Scotland: Land and People**
James McCarthy
ISBN 0 946487 57 X   PB   £7.99

**Wild Scotland**
James McCarthy
ISBN 0 946487 37 5   PB   £8.99

## FOLKLORE

**Tales of the North Coast**
Alan Temperley
ISBN 0 946487 18 9   PB   £8.99

**Tall Tales from an Island**
Peter Macnab
ISBN 0 946487 07 3   PB   £8.99

**Luath Storyteller: Tales of the Picts**
Stuart McHardy
ISBN 1 84282 097 4   PB   £5.99

**Luath Storyteller: Highland Myths and Legends**
George W Macpherson
ISBN 1 84282 064 8   PB   £5.99

## BIOGRAPHY

**Think Global, Act Local: The life and legacy of Sir Patrick Geddes**
Walter Stephen
ISBN 1 84282 079 6 PB £12.99

**Bare Feet and Tackety Boots**
Archie Cameron
ISBN 0 946487 17 0 PB £7.95

**Tobermory Teuchter**
Peter Macnab
ISBN 0 946487 41 3 PB £7.99

**Willie Park Junior: The man who took golf to the world**
Walter Stephen
ISBN 1 905222 21 1 HBK £25.00

## SOCIAL HISTORY

**Crofting Years**
Francis Thompson
ISBN 0 946487 06 5 PB £6.95

**Shale Voices**
Alistair Findlay
ISBN 0 946487 63 4 PB £10.99

## TRAVEL AND LEISURE

**Pilgrims in the Rough: St Andrews beyond the 19th hole**
Michael Tobert
ISBN 0 946487 74 X PB £7.99

## WEDDINGS

**Your Scottish Wedding**
Marianne Rogerson
ISBN 1 905222 24 6 PB £7.99

**The Scottish Wedding Book**
G Wallace Lockhart
ISBN 1 84282 010 9 PB £12.99

Details of these and other Luath books are to be found at **www.luath.co.uk**

## **Luath** Press Limited

*committed to publishing well written books worth reading*

LUATH PRESS takes its name from Robert Burns, whose little collie Luath (*Gael.*, swift or nimble) tripped up Jean Armour at a wedding and gave him the chance to speak to the woman who was to be his wife and the abiding love of his life. Burns called one of 'The Twa Dogs' Luath after Cuchullin's hunting dog in Ossian's *Fingal*. Luath Press was established in 1981 in the heart of Burns country, and is now based a few steps up the road from Burns' first lodgings on Edinburgh's Royal Mile.

Luath offers you distinctive writing with a hint of unexpected pleasures.

Most bookshops in the UK, the US, Canada, Australia, New Zealand and parts of Europe either carry our books in stock or can order them for you. To order direct from us, please send a £sterling cheque, postal order, international money order or your credit card details (number, address of cardholder and expiry date) to us at the address below. Please add post and packing as follows: UK – £1.00 per delivery address; overseas surface mail – £2.50 per delivery address; overseas airmail – £3.50 for the first book to each delivery address, plus £1.00 for each additional book by airmail to the same address. If your order is a gift, we will happily enclose your card or message at no extra charge.

**Luath** Press Limited
543/2 Castlehill
The Royal Mile
Edinburgh EH1 2ND
Scotland
Telephone: 0131 225 4326 (24 hours)
Fax: 0131 225 4324
email: sales@luath.co.uk
Website: www.luath.co.uk